# Essentials of NLP

## 150 Questions & Answers

**InnerPatchPublishing**

# Essentials of NLP

## 150 Questions & Answers

Shlomo Vaknin

**InnerPatchPublishing**

Essentials of NLP: 150 Questions & Answers

Copyright © 2011 by Inner Patch Publishing. All rights reserved.

www.InnerPatchPublishing.com

No part of this publication may be reproduced, stored in a retrieval system, or transmitted in any form or by any means, mechanical, photocopying, electronic, recording, scanning, or otherwise, except as permitted under Section 107 or 108 of the 1976 United States Copyright Act, without the prior written permission of the Publisher. For additional information or requests, please visit our web site.

Limit of Liability/Disclaimer: While the publisher and author have used their best efforts in preparing this book, they make no representations or warranties with respect to the accuracy or completeness of the contents of this book and specifically disclaim any implied warranties of merchantability or fitness for a particular purpose. No warranty may be created or extended by sales representatives or written sales materials. The advice and strategies contained herein may not be suitable for your situation. You should consult with a professional where appropriate. Neither the publisher nor author shall be liable for any loss of profit or any other commercial damages, including but not limited to special, incidental, consequential, or other damages.

For additional copies/bulk purchases of this book in the U.S. or internationally, please contact our sales department at sales@innerpatchpublishing.com

ISBN: 978-965-7489-09-3

Editor: Jonathan Ziegler, M.S.

Cover Design: Natalia Ogneva

Manufactured in the United States of America.

# Thank You

I appreciate your taking the time to read my book.

Now let's get started...

# Other Books By The Author

### The Big Book of NLP, Expanded:
350+ Techniques, Patterns & Strategies

of Neuro Linguistic Programming

### Pain Away:
Advanced Mental Techniques

for Immediate & Long Lasting Relief

### NLP Mastery:
The Meta-Programs

(Practical & Illustrated Guide)

# Contents

| | |
|---|---|
| 1. What is NLP? | 15 |
| 2. What is the basic model of NLP? | 16 |
| 3. But what does NLP actually mean? | 18 |
| 4. What is the Subconscious? | 19 |
| 5. What is a Subliminal? | 21 |
| 6. What is a Representation? | 26 |
| 7. What is an Anchor? | 26 |
| 8. What is Framing? | 28 |
| 9. What is VAK? | 28 |
| 10. What is a State? | 29 |
| 11. What are Association and Dissociation? | 30 |
| 12. What are Parts? | 30 |
| 13. What is Congruence? | 31 |
| 14. What are Subjectivity & Objectivity? | 33 |
| 15. What are the main ideas of General Semantics? | 34 |
| 16. How to I create a Well-Formed Outcome? | 36 |
| 17. What are Cartesian Coordinates? | 42 |
| 18. What are Strategies? | 43 |
| 19. What is the T.O.T.E. Model? | 45 |
| 20. What is the NLP Meta-Model? | 46 |
| 21. What are Meta-Programs? | 49 |
| 22. How Can I Use NLP to Accelerate My Learning and Improve My Skills? | 50 |

| | |
|---|---|
| 23. What are the Learning Levels? | 51 |
| 24. So where do I start? | 53 |
| 25. How NLP analyses mind and behavior to produce results | 55 |
| 26. What is a Representational System? | 56 |
| 27. Well, then, what good are these Rep Systems? | 56 |
| 28. What ARE the Rep Systems? | 57 |
| 29. It might be interesting to a student, but what makes this so valuable to me? | 58 |
| 30. How do I know what Rep System is being used? | 59 |
| 31. What Do I do with a Primary Rep System? | 61 |
| 32. What else can tell me about a person's Rep Systems? | 65 |
| 33. What are the common Eye Accessing Cues? | 65 |
| 34. But is everybody wired like this? | 67 |
| 35. What are Submodalities? | 68 |
| 36. What is the difference between Digital and Analogue Submodalities? | 70 |
| 37. Give me an example. What can I do with Submodalities? | 71 |
| 38. What is Mapping Across? | 73 |
| 39. How do you map across? What is the Swish Pattern? | 74 |
| 40. What is the Godiva Chocolate Pattern? | 76 |
| 41. This is great! What could possibly go wrong? | 78 |
| 42. What are the NLP Presuppositions? | 78 |
| 43. What are Perceptual Positions? | 93 |
| 44. What can I do with Perceptual Positions? | 96 |

| | |
|---|---|
| 45. What is the Perceptual Positions Alignment Pattern? | 97 |
| 46. What happens when Perceptual Positions are not aligned? | 98 |
| 47. What do aligned Perceptual Positions feel like? | 101 |
| 48. How do I know if my Perceptual Positions are not aligned? | 101 |
| 49. How does this work in other perceptual positions? | 104 |
| 50. How do I align my Perceptual Positions? | 106 |
| 51. What is a State? | 112 |
| 52. What is a Mind State? | 113 |
| 53. How can I tell what State I am in? | 113 |
| 54. How can I get control of my State? | 114 |
| 55. What kinds of states should I create? | 115 |
| 56. What other ways can I elicit a state? | 117 |
| 57. How can I apply these skills today? | 119 |
| 58. What is Rapport? | 120 |
| 59. This doesn't sound ethical. Is NLP just manipulation? | 121 |
| 60. What skills should I start with? | 123 |
| 61. How should I practice this? | 124 |
| 62. Then how will I actually create Rapport? | 126 |
| 63. What about posture? | 127 |
| 64. What about movement? | 127 |
| 65. What about breathing? | 128 |
| 66. What is Behavioral Mirroring? | 128 |
| 67. What is Symbolic Mirroring? | 131 |
| 68. What are Exchanged Matches? | 133 |

| | |
|---|---|
| 69. When NOT to Mirror or Match? | 133 |
| 70. But what if someone catches me mimicking them? | 136 |
| 71. How does Anchoring work? | 136 |
| 72. So anchors can be in any sense mode? | 139 |
| 73. Is ice cream an anchor? | 140 |
| 74. How long is an anchor effective? | 142 |
| 75. All this theory is interesting, but how do I do the NLP Anchoring Procedure? | 142 |
| 76. What Is most important to make this work for me? | 144 |
| 77. How can I anchor someone else? | 145 |
| 78. What else can help me anchor effectively? | 147 |
| 79. What is the circle Of Excellence Pattern? | 147 |
| 80. What is the Collapsing Anchors Pattern? | 150 |
| 81. What is the Change Personal History Pattern? | 152 |
| 82. How do you chain anchors? | 155 |
| 83. What else can I do with anchors? | 158 |
| 84. What is the Visual Squash Pattern? | 159 |
| 85. How do I use Framing? | 162 |
| 86. What is the "As If" Frame? | 164 |
| 87. How to apply Framing for Fear of Rejection or Criticism? | 166 |
| 88. What Is the NLP Phobia Cure Pattern? | 168 |
| 89. What are Dilts' Logical Levels? | 169 |
| 90. So what do we do about the phobia? | 173 |
| 91. What about Modeling? | 176 |
| 92. What are the key elements of modeling? | 180 |

| | |
|---|---|
| 93. Once you have a model, what do you do with it? | 184 |
| 94. What is the NLP Meta-Model Of Language? | 184 |
| 95. What are Generalizations? | 188 |
| 96. What are Universal Quantifiers? | 189 |
| 97. What are Lost Performatives? | 190 |
| 98. What are Modal Operators? | 191 |
| 99. What are Deletions? | 192 |
| 100. What is Lack of Referential Index? | 194 |
| 101. What are Comparative Deletions? | 195 |
| 102. What are Distortions? | 195 |
| 103. What is Nominalization? | 196 |
| 104. What is Mind Reading? | 198 |
| 105. What are Cause and Effect Distortions? | 199 |
| 106. What are Presuppositions? | 200 |
| 107. What is Complex Equivalence? | 201 |
| 108. How can I use the Meta-Model for therapy? | 202 |
| 109. What is The Milton Model? | 204 |
| 110. Why use Hypnosis in NLP? | 205 |
| 111. Who was Milton Erickson? | 205 |
| 112. What is Hypnosis? | 207 |
| 113. What is a Trance? | 208 |
| 114. If Rapid, Brief Trance is Really Possible, Show Me One. | 209 |
| 115. What is Conversational Hypnosis? | 211 |
| 116. What about the role of the Subconscious in hypnosis? | 211 |

| | |
|---|---|
| 117. What is the Milton Model good for? | 212 |
| 118. What is Transderivational Search? | 213 |
| 119. How can I actually use the Milton Model? | 214 |
| 120. What are Meta-Model Violations? | 215 |
| 121. What is Pacing Current Experience? | 215 |
| 122. What are Pacing and Leading? | 216 |
| 123. What are Linking Words? | 217 |
| 124. What is Disjunction? | 218 |
| 125. What are Implied Causes? | 220 |
| 126. What are Tag Questions? | 221 |
| 127. What are Double Binds? | 222 |
| 128. What are Embedded Commands? | 222 |
| 129. What is Analogue Marking? | 223 |
| 130. What is Utilization? | 223 |
| 131. What is Nesting? | 225 |
| 132. What are Extended Quotes? | 226 |
| 133. Spell Out Words? | 227 |
| 134. What is Conversational Postulate? | 227 |
| 135. What are Selectional Restriction Violations? | 228 |
| 136. What are Ambiguities? | 228 |
| 137. What are Phonological Ambiguities? | 229 |
| 138. What are Syntactic Ambiguities? | 229 |
| 139. What are Scope Ambiguities? | 230 |
| 140. What are Punctuation Ambiguities? | 231 |
| 141. What is a Metaphor? | 231 |
| 142. What is the Satir Model? | 234 |

| | |
|---|---|
| 143. What are the Satir Categories? | 234 |
| 144. Who is The Blamer? | 235 |
| 145. Who is The Placater? | 236 |
| 146. Who is The Computer? | 237 |
| 147. Who is The Distracter? | 238 |
| 148. Who is The Leveler? | 239 |
| 149. What about Flexibility? | 239 |
| 150. What is Category Rapport-Building? | 240 |
| • One more: Why isn't NLP a mainstream approach? | 244 |
| • What else? | 248 |

# What is NLP?

NLP stands for **neuro-linguistic programming**. NLP teaches us to create excellence and offers you a wealth of skills for that purpose.

**John Grinder** and **Richard Bandler** developed NLP in the early 1970's. John Grinder was a professor of linguistics at UC Santa Cruz while Richard Bandler was a student of computing and mathematics. They worked with ingenious, talented and successful people to turn NLP into an important and useful method of training for people from all walks of life.

People use NLP in their everyday relationships and they use it to achieve success in everything from sales to sports. As a professor of linguistics, Grinder was very interested in the connections between language, the mind, and behavior. Bandler had a true gift for a key NLP skill called modeling. One of the questions that they pursued had to do with successful therapists. Why, they wondered, was it that in a particular technique of psychotherapy, a few therapists stood out as being highly effective?

What was the difference that made the difference? This got them interested in analyzing everything about these therapists. From this early vision, NLP grew into a rich field of analysis, techniques, and training that has been applied to many varied professional and personal pursuits.

# What is the basic model of NLP?

The basic model of NLP IS to model, that is, to do as other successful people do. NLP helps you achieve excellence by modeling how others have achieved excellence. If you want to become the best golfer in the world, NLP can help you do that. If you want to be the highest-paid sales person, NLP can help you do that. NLP can do that, because there are people who have already achieved the kinds of things you want to achieve. NLP unlocks THEIR secrets to unlock YOUR potential.

But NLP gives us MORE than that. NLP practitioners have modeled many, many people. We know that excellent people have certain things in common, things that drive their success. These excellent people have ways to motivate themselves and motivate other people to achieve great things. They know how to establish a good connection with people, and that helps them be a fantastic manager, psychotherapist, or sales person. They have ways to bounce back from rough times and create incredible momentum for success. NLP has ways to turn challenges into motivation as if challenges were jet fuel.

But NLP gives us even more than THAT. Some of the most important models that NLP has created are not just what to do, but HOW to change. NLP has many ways for you to create or change behavior. That means that if you want to give a talk to a large group of people, but start shaking in fear whenever you think of it, you can use NLP to become a person who loves to give talks, a person who really feels GOOD giving talks, even to become a person who strives to give talks to the largest audience possible.

NLP creates this kind of personal change. It eliminates obstacles, it restores and builds energy, and it brings your motivations into alignment like a laser beam, burning through life's obstacles.

Let's take this one step farther. NLP means even more than how to change. It shows us how to get the knowledge, how to get the techniques and how to expand and express our curiosity. Sure, there are techniques that you can apply right now, and this training has plenty of them, but NLP provides much more than a cookbook. NLP encourages discovery.

Every new challenge can become an opportunity to take things to another level. Every new client or customer can become a person that will teach you something more about personal change and success. A spirit of curiosity gives you all you need to begin. The willingness to experiment takes you toward mastery. The intention to create fantastic outcomes turns that mastery into success. NLP amazes people, because you can use it to amplify those precious ingredients. You are in for a true adventure.

# But what does NLP actually mean?

The **neuro** in neuro-linguistic programming refers to our nervous system, including the brain. You could say neuro refers to how our body handles our experiences. You can feel great, you can have a traumatic reaction, you can be depressed or you can be highly motivated, depending on how your nervous system handles your experiences.

Your experiences include all the senses, including symbols like words. That explains why **linguistic** appears in neurolinguistic. Linguistic, a word related to language, refers to how symbols affect us. When a personal coach helps us become motivated, they use words to affect our nervous system.

The word **programming** appears in neurolinguistic programming because NLP uses symbols and experiences in the best possible way to achieve excellence. You can program your nervous system to bring out successful thinking and behavior that goes way beyond what you could do without these methods.

NLP uses very smart techniques to improve our reactions to the challenges of life. This way, we feel motivated to take on the challenges that matter most. We can actually shrink the size of the challenges while we grow our abilities. This training will tell you exactly how to do that, and much more.

# What is the Subconscious?

The subconscious mind contains everything in your mind that you are not aware of. Some of these things are easy to become aware of.

Stop and listen to the sounds around you that you weren't aware of until...

**now**.

Some of these things you can directly influence, like if your fidgeting without knowing it and someone asks you to stop.

You can even influence some of them indirectly, like when you learn relaxation or stress management, and lower your heart rate or brain activity. This brings up an interesting point. Where should you draw the **boundary** between the subconscious mind and the mechanics of the body, such as the electric impulses and chemical reactions that regulate the heartbeat? Since NLP has evolved into a holistic approach, it thinks of the body and mind as an interplay or an entity, not as two things with a definite line between them.

The mind can have extraordinary effects on the body. Countless research studies have shown this. NLP has hundreds of patterns- far more than you could possibly need to be an effective practitioner- that can alter your state. There's even one for allergies. All aspects of you are connected. This point of view empowers you.

And please remember that we used the word "**influence**." There's no reason to feel guilty if you get sick, as if you have total control over every aspect of your body. We call NLP a practice because you can learn and improve your use of NLP over your entire lifetime. Some people get carried away, like a person who said not to talk about personal growth using the word growth, because that would give you cancer. That's definitely getting carried away. They probably said that because subtle word choices can have a big effect on how people perform. We will be learning a lot of powerful language patterns in this book. Words will become your allies in creating powerful skills for a more fulfilling life.

Among its many jobs, the subconscious mind decides what needs to become conscious, what you can do subconsciously, and what your mental filters can dispose of. Neuropsychologists have even found a physical area of the brain that serves to filter your sensory impressions. It allows you to focus on what you need to do, but if it detects possible danger, it directs your attention to it. The subconscious mind performs many such tasks, so a lot of our behavior gets shaped by things we don't think about. This can happen in unwanted ways as well.

Just as animal trainers shape the behavior of tigers, dogs, and dolphins in complicated ways, our behavior has been shaped without our knowledge. Our patterns of experience, our temperament, and even programming by commercial advertisers influence us.

The subconscious can actually put up barriers to awareness in the form of psychological defenses; NLP provides the antidote. It puts the tools of behavioral change in your hands to use according to your values. It helps you restore awareness where you need it. Better yet, it can be a lot of fun to use NLP, and it can create plenty of inspiration in your life. For example, people can get into a lot of hang-ups, avoiding things that they would be better off dealing with. NLP can make it easier for people to be assertive and proactive in their lives, because it can open up a positive pathway to action.

This way, the subconscious mind does not busy itself so much putting up obstacles or defenses. Anxiety gets reduced, and the person becomes reconnected with their joys, passions, and higher values. When people switch on this way, they are much more successful and attractive.

# What is a Subliminal?

Subliminal refers to things that you do not consciously perceive. Although you don't perceive subliminals, they may have an effect on you. People have a lot of misunderstandings about subliminals. In the 1950's, an advertising consultant claimed that he could get people to buy more popcorn or soft drinks by flashing images of those items during a movie, or by flashing words commanding them to buy the items. He later admitted that he had made it up, and other researchers discovered that it couldn't be done with his techniques. However, researchers have shown that subliminals work in other ways that we can put to good use in NLP. NLP practitioners, and people that NLP has modeled, have effectively made use of subliminals.

People have various ways to make something subliminal. For example, they can make it appear too briefly or too dim for anyone to perceive it consciously, or produce a sound so quiet that no one can consciously hear it. Psychological researchers can flash words so quickly that no one consciously sees the words, yet those unseen words or images can affect people.

Another kind of subliminal, the kind commonly used in NLP, uses words or body language in a way that the person does not perceive, because they do not pay attention to it. This kind of subliminal is not invisible because you could consciously perceive it, if you paid special attention. This kind of subliminal does however evade your conscious awareness. The speaker makes this possible by keeping your conscious mind busy paying attention to something else, or by getting you into trance, where you have little, if any, conscious mind to perceive anything with. Many magic tricks also work in this same way.

The famous hypnotherapist Milton Erickson has given us many ways to use subliminal communication. For example, he used something called embedded commands, where words that form part of a sentence provide their own secret message. This is an example of how you can create subliminal messages with ambiguity. If you say something with two possible meanings, the person may not perceive the meaning that provokes their defenses.

However, they will perceive the other message that does not provoke their defenses. Nevertheless, that message, the one that they aren't consciously aware of, can have a real impact.

Subliminals can't exert their influence with the strength of full commands or complicated messages. Subliminal recordings don't work in the way they are typically advertised. However, you can use subliminals as part of an approach that uses state management to get results. Subliminals create more subtle effects than the old -fashioned subliminal recordings that people started creating back in the 1950's.

In advertising, they have discovered that if something feels familiar to you, then you will prefer it over something you don't feel so familiar with. This happens even though you only got the feeling because you were exposed to the thing through a subliminal source, such as a brief image, or something you didn't notice that appeared in a movie.

We want to make this point clear: a subliminal image or idea gets into the brain, but not into conscious awareness.

This is like the difference between hardness and pitch or color. A coin has a certain hardness, whether you perceive the hardness or not. But color as we perceive it has the property of color because of three different light-sensing organs in the eyes that the brain uses to construct color. Dogs perceive color much differently than we do.

The same thing applies to the pitch of a musical note. The difference in wave lengths of two low pitches and two high pitches may sound like the same difference, but the actual difference, if you count the waves, turns out to be much larger between the higher notes. We are pointing out that perception and effect are two different things. You don't need to be aware of something in order for it to affect your state of mind.

Let's return to the idea of things that have a subliminal effect simply because the person does not notice them. Consider product placements in the media. Even though people don't usually consciously notice product placements in movies and TV shows, advertisers spend enormous amounts of money to get product placements. This provides an example of something that COULD be consciously perceived, but acts as a subliminal by going unnoticed- or at least un-featured. Similarly, you'll notice that TV commercials don't usually give you a lot of information about a product. Instead, they give you impressions, feelings, and exposure.

Subliminals can also do something called priming. You can use subliminals to amplify a person's emotional needs or other states. This doesn't control them like a robot, but it does increase the odds that they will do something that EXPRESSES that state. For example, psychological research has shown that people are more likely to act secure and well adjusted when the researchers prime them with positive, secure messages such as "mommy and I are one." It may seem unbelievable that "mommy and I are one" could have an effect on people, but researchers have built up a good body of research using this very phrase.

Notice the primitive nature of the phrase "mommy and I are one". Subliminals exert their influence with a few words, a very simple idea, or just an image. This happens because subliminals don't appeal directly to the more complex areas of the mind; they appeal to the primitive areas.

Even when, as with words, the subliminal message requires processing by higher brain areas for initial interpretation, they still exert their influence through the more primitive parts of the brain. When a message or experience primes people to feel more secure in some way, psychology calls this "secure base priming". Unfortunately, people who know how to control the masses use priming, but they attack the secure base. This causes people to act out of fear. This can get a population to go along with starting wars or discriminating against minorities.

It can make people hyper-vigilant, that is, overly alert to possible danger, so they are more likely to watch news that covers alarming things.

Viewers are so important to TV stations that the news broadcasts will go to great lengths, even creating false impressions. For example, a news organization in Denver, Colorado broadcast a series of stories about violence Denver called "the summer of violence". However, Denver actually had less violence that summer.

The station used a cynical, manipulative way to get people to watch. In contrast, NLP serves to produce excellence wherever it can, not to steal peoples' time with dishonesty.

# What is a Representation?

The word "**representation**" refers to how we represent things in our minds. If you think of a chair, it has a certain representation. Did you think of a **wooden** chair? Was it **padded**? What **color** was it? All these representations belong to you.

Someone else will think of a different chair. This becomes very important when we pursue excellence, because our representations can help or hinder us. As we go along in this course, you will discover very helpful ways to make your representations far more useful.

We don't just represent objects in our minds; **we represent ideas and values**. How your mind represents them has a great impact on your motivation, behavior, and effect on others.

# What is an Anchor?

We are not talking about boats here. In NLP, **we use anchors to get into the right state of mind for doing something.** In order to have an anchor, you have to connect a symbol with a desired state of mind. You can create an especially powerful symbol by using a point on your body that you touch, or a way that you position your fingers. If, every time you feel confident, you make an okay sign with your non-dominant hand, you can help generate confidence by making that okay sign.

We call this triggering the state. When you use an anchor to trigger the state, you are firing the anchor. When you form the okay sign, you are firing the anchor. If it works, you have triggered the state.

Anchors are used all sorts of ways in NLP. They can even be used subconsciously. Coaches have used an uncomfortable anchor in order to stop clients from interfering with therapy. Grinder talks about a client who was afraid of snakes. She had a habit of obstructing what needed to happen in her coaching session.

Grinder told her that he had seen snakes actually going right across the floor, and he tracked his eyes across the floor behind her. From that time, whenever the woman started obstructing, he would track his eyes across the floor behind her. She didn't notice that this was happening, but it still changed her behavior.

In this case, his eye movement was the anchor. When he fired the anchor, that is, made the eye tracking movement, he triggered some discomfort in her. This discomfort then became connected to her obstructing behavior and not only interrupted it, but caused it to occur less frequently.

# What is Framing?

While anchoring uses the more primitive side of the nervous system, framing works through communication and thinking. The word "frame" refers to the assumptions that shape how you perceive something and what choices you think you have. You've heard the expression "frame of mind" but in NLP, frames serve more as frames of reality. We all put a frame around reality, meaning we exclude a lot of reality. If we didn't, we'd have too much reality and blow a fuse. So NLP doesn't get rid of our frames, it turns framing into an art and a science. But, first, realize what your frame includes and excludes. People don't usually know their own frames any more than a fish knows about water.

Frames often limit us too much. Develop the ability to step outside of the frame, and you gain a very valuable skill, especially in organizations, where a frame can limit an entire group of people. When you step outside of the frame, you see the hidden opportunities. You've heard the expression "think outside of the box." It refers to the same thing.

# What is VAK?

We use three primary senses to learn and communicate. VAK refers to them. They include **visual** (seeing), **auditory** (hearing) and **kinesthetic** (feeling/

movement). NLP practitioners observe that they can improve their connection with others and create more effective excellence strategies by paying attention to which sense modes a person uses. Educators have explored the idea that each student can benefit from emphasizing one sense mode over the others, depending on the sense they use most to gain information.  Later in the training, we teach you to use these sense modes in practical ways.

# What is a State?

A state is the sum total of everything about you at a given time. You can sum up a state as being distraught, joyful, excited, or any other emotion. But a state contains more than emotion.

**States tend to make certain abilities more accessible.** Think creatively about a problem, and you cultivate a creative state; your creative resources come into play. Psychology uses the word **"kindling"** to describe how a resource sort of catches fire from this kind of activation encouraging it to come fully into action.

Since people can be stuck in a dysfunctional state, NLP has techniques to stop these states so that the person can move into a more appropriate state. NLP calls this **"breaking state"**. It resembles what people try to do when they say, "Snap out of it." NLP processes use breaking state, as you will experience first-hand during this training.

# What are Association and Dissociation?

**Dissociation** means being disconnected from your normal consciousness and center of self. A little dissociation can reduce your discomfort and add some objectivity when you deal with a difficult issue in an NLP experience.

**Association** means being connected to your experience, being fully aware of your sensations, thoughts and feelings and being very subjective. This is also called "first hand" experience.

People who can't control their own dissociation, because of a problem such as a brain injury, can feel very disconnected from reality at times, kind of like being in a fog. This keeps the parts of a person's personality from working well together. In fact, NLP has processes that help people get their personality to work more as a single, aligned force.

# What are Parts?

The word "parts" refers to clusters of values, motivations, and other personality traits that tend to work together, a little bit like a personality. In fact, some people call them sub-personalities. People with a lot of dissociation may have their parts act as full-blown alternative personalities, as in multiple personalities, known as dissociative identity disorder. But for most people, having parts works pretty well.

Different situations call for different parts to come to the foreground or activate. Parts relate to states. If you get into the right state for a challenge, this helps bring the most appropriate parts forward. Consider playfulness. Let's say you are on a vacation and having a lot of fun at the beach. There, your personality contrasts quite a bit with your personality at work; the beach does not activate your worries, your workplace knowledge, nor your serious side. You are giving that aspect of yourself a rest and just having fun. NLP works with parts to align you for making a good decision, handling a challenge, or communicating well. Sometimes NLP will even help your parts negotiate.

# What is Congruence?

Alignment, as occurs when your parts are aligned, brings much value to NLP, because it empowers our resources. The most basic alignment occurs when our sense modalities are in harmony. On a larger scale, we become congruent when our parts harmonize. If there is a mismatch, then we have internal contradiction. As you'll recall, parts act like little personalities within us, or clusters of motivations that work together. And ecology refers to parts or other systems supporting each other. So you could say that in congruence, your parts play well together.

On an even grander level, congruence happens when our alignment points in a constructive direction that matches our self-interest. The highest order of congruence takes place when we align all the way up to and include our higher values and aspirations. This extreme alignment brings perhaps the greatest satisfaction a human being can experience.

When you meet someone who is not congruent, that is incongruent, they tend to say things that don't quite match up, or their behavior doesn't match what they say, or their outcomes don't match what they are trying to do. If you explore this with someone who is incongruent, they will reveal deeper and more obvious incongruities and deeper mis-matches.

They may show ambivalence about the results they say they want. They may get a lot of benefits from the status quo of just saying they want to change. They may reveal insecurities about what they are trying to do. They may somehow dislike the kind of person they say they are trying to meet, like maybe feeling angry with all members of the opposite sex.

They may have mental health or neurological problems that they have not fully accepted or learned to cope with. They might deny their serious problems with alcohol or other drugs. The list goes on. Many things can cause incongruence.

If you are consulting or coaching someone who has some kind of incongruity, you will want to use NLP strategies that help this person resolve these mismatches.

We call this ability to get parts to mesh well "reintegration". Alignment provides the foundation of NLP. Alignment makes personal excellence and healing possible.

# What are Subjectivity & Objectivity?

NLP thrives on results. NLP strives to produce excellence. NLP pays attention to how people interpret their experiences, so that it can tailor its approach to the individual. NLP can help you have a more meaningful and useful subjective world.

That means the world as you interpret or experience it. Subjectivity means your personal take on what happens; how you react to things internally.

By **objectivity**, we mean the verifiable information that we can actually account for like historical or scientific facts.

General semantics provides part of the foundation of NLP. NLP practitioners sum it up with the quote from Alfred Korzybski, **"The map is not the territory."**

NLP and general semantics understand that our capacity for language not only provides value, but also creates traps. Language has a great effect on our thinking, so it serves as a powerful tool that can cause a lot of damage as well as good.

# What are the main ideas of General Semantics?

General semantics tells us that our nervous systems, culture, and language limit our ability to perceive reality. It supports scientific thinking, in the sense that we test our beliefs in order to refine them. The language traps that general semantics points out provide a great introduction to general semantics.

One is that, in order to speak or write, we must misrepresent the world. That's because we can't communicate or even perceive everything. That means that we must be both factual AND artificial in how we communicate.

Another trap is that we make things more artificial or inaccurate by thinking in polarities such as "You are either with me or against me," or "it's either right or wrong" as though there were no shades of gray.

We also misuse the word "is", like when we say, "he IS a criminal," as though that were all that he is, not also a person, son, etc.

"Are you a criminal?" If you have ever gone over the speed limit or left some income off of your taxes, should you answer yes to this question? Surely that would be misleading, as you are more than just a criminal. Instead of calling someone a zealot, think of what would happen if you said, "I'm disturbed about your zealotry." This gives the two of you something to talk about besides whether the person IS a zealot. Who knows? You BOTH might learn something.

Notice that, in the sentence, "I'm disturbed about your zealotry," we got rid of the word IS. Realizing that variations of the verb **to be** (like **is**, **was**, and **are**) force us to find other, more honest and realistic ways to speak. This resulted in a version of English called **E-prime**.

Try writing something without any version of the verb "to be" and see what happens. We aren't purists, but we wrote a good deal of this course in E-prime. You'll find that propaganda makes much heavier use of the verb "to be" than other writing. The U.S. Constitution has a low usage. And, without the verb "to be", it's harder to lie.

Another language trap happens when we treat abstract ideas and opinions as though they were actual things in the world. People do this so much, that, in a very real sense, they're living in a fantasy world.

General semantics provided the basis for the NLP meta-model. When we get into the meta-model, we'll cover some wonderful tools that you can use in everyday communication, as well as in leadership, sales, and even therapy.

# How to I create a Well-Formed Outcome?

Goals can go a long way in helping you achieve excellence. Your goal may be to have a great time at a party, or become a billionaire within three years. There are many different kinds of goals.

If you want to achieve your goal, NLP offers you a pattern to form a very specific, detailed kind of goal called a well-formed outcome.

NLP developers have come up with a well-formed outcome that they designed to get your conscious and subconscious minds working together in a powerful way. The well-formed outcome also gives you details and accountability that a goal needs so that you can achieve it.

The well-formed outcome has these factors:

**First: In Positive Terms: What do I want?**

Start with the question, "What do I want?" Too many people don't really stop and ask this question. They pick up all sorts of ideas about what they want. These ideas come from what everybody else seems to want, or from their parents, or from commercials.

Too many people put their focus on what they don't want. Unfortunately, this can reduce their creativity and their connection with their values. NLP combats this, placing your focus on the positive.

You know you have answered the question "What do I want?" when you feel like you have really connected with the answer; like you have really dropped down into a grounded place and KNOW; or you have achieved something more than just excitement, but a real sense of fulfillment.

To answer the question "What do I want?", keep working on your answer until you have stated it in 100% positive terms. This really helps build your motivation. While you're at it, keep on adding details. Get the details by thinking about when and where the outcome will take place, who is involved, and about what it will mean to you when it takes place.

When you envision the achievement of the outcome, you can see it from the point of view of an observer. By placing the success scene outside of yourself, you turn this outcome into one that you must pursue. This psychological trick helps give your subconscious mind dogged persistence and excitement.

**Second: Transform the Answer into Sense-Based Language**

Convert your answer from question number one, "What Do You Want?" into sense-based language. Describe your outcome in terms of what you can see, touch, feel, taste, and smell. This helps to connect you with what you want, it helps you define your goals more precisely, and it helps you encourage your subconscious mind to support you with it's powers of motivation and creativity.

A question that helps answer this is, "How will you

know when you get there?" or, "What evidence will tell you that you achieved your outcome?" The question can also motivate you, because it catapults you into that future, where you have achieved your outcome. Answer the question with very concrete things, that is, things that you can see, hear, and touch.

### Third: Self-Initiated and Self-Controlled

Ask, for each part of the outcome, "How am I connected with this outcome through things that I directly cause?" Some of your outcomes may be things that you do not directly do. For example, you can't use magic to force investors to give you lots of money. But you can come close, by developing a compelling presentation, a successful management team, and top-notch charisma.

Asking this question, "How am I connected to this outcome through things that I directly cause?" This will take you into the accountability zone. If the outcome is under your control, then you can become more confident about it. Of course, the further you put the outcome into the future or the bigger you make the outcome, the more you will have to influence others through leadership. You may have to find your way around obstacles that you cannot directly eliminate. Of course, the bigger you make your plans, the more you will deal with challenges.

A fellow who wanted to raise funds for prostate cancer experienced complete rejection by the very organization he wanted to raise money for. Why? Because he had a weird idea. But, he went ahead with his idea and raised more than ten times the amount of money than the organization raised. He couldn't control the organization, and he couldn't control the people who gave the money, but he could control his ability to communicate. And he could control his mustache.

His weird idea? To create buzz by asking men to grow a mustache for prostate cancer. He started his idea in Australia, and it spread from there. Note that he stayed focused on what he could control, and did not allow rejection to deter him; he did not allow what he could not control to stop him. With what he could control, he created influence; influence that created a phenomenon way beyond anyone's expectations, even his.

**Fourth: Contextualize the Outcome**

Round out your outcome by asking when and where it should take place. In other words, describe the circumstances of your outcome. In whose presence should it occur? Is it ongoing, or just at certain times? This begins to place your outcome into the larger ecology of your needs and the systems you are to deal with. It also brings your vision more to life for both your conscious and subconscious minds. As you give your outcome context, include the various demands and sacrifices that come with the goal. In this successful scenario, how have the energy, staff, time and other resources been deployed?

**Fifth: Secondary Gain and Ecology**

Personal ecology means that you consider your personal needs, aspirations, and values in the outcome. Personal ecology gives an important edge to your plans because it brings about inner alignment. If any part of you feels at all uncomfortable with the outcome, then you should add, remove, or improve whatever aspects of your outcome needed to eliminate this discomfort. Once you're totally on board, in other words, once you have your motivations fully aligned, then you have put yourself in a much better position to succeed. Personal alignment provides a powerful force.

You can also take a look at the flip side of this question. What is there about the status quo that might give you a reason to stay stuck? Might your subconscious mind have any reasons to jinx your plans?

You should definitely address any problems like that in your outcome. And everyone, no matter how strong their will or how smart or courageous, has incentives not to move forward with their plans. Dealing with this now aligns the forces of your personality for success.

**Sixth: Resources**

Ask yourself, "Do I have all the resources I need to achieve my outcome?"

Ask, "Are the costs and consequences of obtaining this outcome acceptable?

Your plans are too important NOT to be realistic about. Every idea has its costs and sacrifices. Every idea involves consequences that deserve consideration. When you're excited, you may rush ahead to later discover dire consequences. Pure excitement does not create excellence all by itself.

Take a sober look at the costs and consequences in balance with the desired outcome. You may need to do some out-of-the-box thinking to dial in your outcome in the face of these real-world considerations. You can adjust your outcome and plans to build in the necessary resources, and to build in the steps to those resources.

A well-formed outcome is your early investment in achievement. **As you think through the path to your outcome, what will you need along the way?**

This is a good place to use mind mapping, where you map out all the resources that connect with your outcome, and then all the means you might use to get those resources in place, on time and on budget. And we aren't just talking about money and objects. Resources can include "soft resources" like connections, good will, time, and knowledge.

### Seventh: Whole System Ecology

You have already started thinking about your personal ecology. There are other individuals and systems as well. By systems, we mean families, schools, regulatory government agencies, businesses and so on. Does your outcome, as defined so far, impair your relationship with any other individuals or systems? What can you do about it?

Ask the helpful question, "If I could have it now, would I take it?"

Maybe the answer is obvious, but this question really gets you thinking about possible downsides or imperfections in your outcome. The question, "If I could have it now, would I take it?" can inspire you to evolve your outcome. Of course, nobody wants paralysis by analysis, but don't under-think your outcome.

Put your mind into that outcome as if you have achieved it, and open your thinking to means of improving that outcome. The time to rework your outcomes comes before you start investing a lot of resources. The way to align with your highest goals is to stay flexible about your outcome, to rework the outcome as needed and to shape the outcome into something even better. Now you are developing one of the hallmarks of NLP: ecology; where all parts of you agree with the outcome; where your desires, your values, and your needs are all aligned into one powerful direction.

# What are Cartesian Coordinates?

You can apply Cartesian coordinates to decisions in order to check your ecology and refine your outcomes. You can try this on a decision you're considering.

Here they are:

**If I do X, what will happen?**

**If I do X, what won't happen?**

**If I don't do X, what will happen?**

**If I don't do X, what won't happen?**

Note anything that you hadn't thought of, or any way that these questions help you put things into perspective.

# What are Strategies?

A strategy is the approach you take to getting a result such as solving a problem or succeeding at something. It can even be the way you make a decision, form an opinion, or get a creative idea. NLP is very interested in the strategies that successful people use to BE successful.

Sometimes NLP analysis finds many strategies, and must experiment to figure out which ones are really effective; which ones really make a difference.

Strategies can be as obvious as a written plan of action, or as subtle as how you subconsciously use submodalities to make a decision.

NLP offers five primary categories for strategies, based on what they are intended for:

1. **Decision strategies**, or how we make a decision,

2. **Motivation strategies**, or how we get motivated to do something,

3. **Reality strategies,** or how we form our opinions,

4. **Learning strategies**, or how we learn to do something,

5. **Memory strategies**, or how we recall what we have learned or experienced

You can analyze your own strategies and compare

them to others.

For example, compare the way your shop for clothes with someone of the opposite sex.

Which strategy saves time? How? Which saves money? How?

Which gets the most attractive clothes? How?

Which strategies are mutually exclusive, for example, is the money-saving strategy at odds with getting attractive clothes?

As we get deeper into analyzing strategies, you'll see how our rep systems form essential parts of strategies, but can all be changed, often with very helpful and liberating results.

Do you remember that these rep systems include things such as your self-talk, how you feel, and how you imagine future situations? You will see examples of strategies when we discuss modeling and other aspects of NLP. When we go into creating well-formed outcomes, strategies will figure importantly. Strategy analysis forms much of modeling. We also look at dysfunctional strategies and how to respond to them, whether we do so to keep our own sanity, or to help someone else be more successful. For this, we actually design new strategies.

**The NLP T.O.T.E. model is a strategy.**

# What is the T.O.T.E. Model?

The T.O.T.E. model is perhaps the most basic strategy for guiding human behavior. It stands for **test, operate, test, exit,** so it sounds like a simple computer program. It means that you check to see if you have the result you want (that's the test), and if not, do something to get the result (that's when you operate), test again to see if you got the result, and keep going through that test and operate cycle until you get the result. That's when you stop trying to get the result, or exit.

Breaking behavior down into this basic unit helps you understand and create more complicated strategies. T.O.T.E. supports modeling. NLP calls each T.O.T.E. strategy a Tote.

Since the Tote cycles through a checking and acting loop, it can be broken if the person is not persistent. Giving up is another Tote. The test might come in the form of, "Do I feel too uncomfortable to persist?" Then the operation is to go for the outcome. If it makes the person feel too uncomfortable, they somehow experience this (remember that is the test part), and give up, or, in TOTE language, exit.

As you can see, there can be any number of Totes going on all at the same time. You can even think of them as going all the way down to your most basic physiology, as your body adjusts countless things like your temperature, heart rate, and blood sugar, based on feedback that triggers a physiological Tote. That is called homeostasis. This idea comes from cybernetics, one of the foundations of NLP.

# What is the NLP Meta-Model?

The meta-model is a way to create questions that move you from less specific statements toward the specific sensory experiences that the statement came from. You could say it serves to help people become more responsible for where their thoughts come from.

For example, if a person forms their opinions from vaguely recalled images and headlines from the media, you know that this happily brainwashed person resembles the people in Orwell's novel 1984.

The meta-model comes from NLP's ability to get a bird's-eye view of what is going on. The Meta-Model looks at how we create a mental map of reality. In order to make a real map, you know you have to dispense with much of the available information.

Stephen Wright jokes that he has a full-scale map of the United States. He says last summer he folded it.

If he wants that map in his glove compartment, then he'll need to get one with less information, just like we do when we form our mental maps.

In order for us to create mental maps, we have to delete or distort the available information. Another way of putting it is that we have to filter or encode it.

If you see a house painted white, you would say it was a white house. But if you didn't see it from all sides, you're assuming all the sides are white. Of course, if we didn't delete information our brains would be overwhelmed, so it is necessary. What it comes down to is whether we are doing it in an effective way or not.

The art of applying the Meta-Model is in bringing dysfunctional deletions, distortions and generalizations to awareness in order to bring in valuable but overlooked information.

Part of NLP's job is to examine how people create their maps. NLP looks for problems such as overgeneralizing. Bigotry is a nasty form, of overgeneralization.

If I say that all French people are rude, I'd be overgeneralizing.

If I said many French people are tired of silly tourists, I might at least be less of a generalization. But I'd still be telling only part of the story.

Where do poor maps of reality come from? Genetics provides one answer. We are genetically programmed to think of our group as being superior, and to feel aggressive towards a different group. Anthropologists estimate that tribal civilizations generally had incredibly high death rates because of ongoing tribal warfare.

Other sources of poor maps include rules we

subconsciously get from our families and society, and our own psychological defense mechanisms and temperaments. When people suffer from depression, many of them also experience very different thought patterns such as negative thoughts about themselves that were not typical of them before they became depressed.

Examples of deletions, generalizations, and distortions, as well as responses that highlight them can help us understand the Meta-Model.

Here is an example of uncovering an overgeneralization. If I say, "All Germans make love loudly," you might say, "I had no idea you were such a voyeur. Where did you get the time to listen to them all?"

Now, let's look at an unspecified relationship.

If I say, "I won't really feel like a man until I have a nice car," an NLP practitioner might say, "How have you felt like a man since you haven't had a nice car?"

I suppose we could get a little cheeky and take this to another level.

You could say to the practitioner, "Silly practitioner, didn't you know that the phrase 'I won't really feel like a man' is an idiom for, 'I'm neurotic'?"

The practitioner might reply, "And my fees are an idiom for, 'I'm very effective at what I do.'"

# What are Meta-Programs?

Meta-programs are the master programs that manage our mental processes. The meta-model helps us make the connection between thoughts and the sensory representations that they come from. Meta-programs are what we find when we analyze the rules that determine who we select from our experiences to form our patterns of thinking and decision making.

This perspective comes from cybernetics, an important influence that shaped NLP. You could say that a thermostat has rules that control when the air conditioning or heating turn on and off. In that sense, the thermostat's rules are meta-programs.

Meta-programs determine what strategy a person uses or even creates in order to accomplish something. As you know, strategies are the method someone uses to get a result, even an internal result such as making a decision.

The "toward versus away from" meta-program gives us a great way to improve how we communicate, so we'll use it as an example as some people are motivated by moving toward a result.

If they plan on doing their taxes, the may be motivated by the process, by desire for a sense of mastery, or by the relief they will feel dropping the envelope in the mail.

If the away from style motivates the person, they

will focus on avoiding trouble with the government, and getting the whole thing over with so they don't have to suffer through it any longer than necessary. If you want to motivate someone, you need to know if they use a **toward** or **away from** meta-program.

# How Can I Use NLP to Accelerate My Learning and Improve My Skills?

This special section on learning shows you a valuable way to apply what you now know about NLP. In this section, you will use NLP to accelerate your learning and build your skills more rapidly.

As you now know, NLP is about modeling excellent people and transferring those skills to others. This is a major reason that NLP has gotten deep into the subject of learning and skill development. NLP people wanted to know who had the best teaching expertise and what methods where doing the best job of accelerating learning. Not only did NLP help popularize some accelerated learning methods, it also helps it's own students learn NLP.

One way NLP helps is by training you to understand and work with representational systems, our sense modes, as you will see. One of the most important things educational research is telling us is that translating learning activities and information into all three modes of seeing, hearing and feeling is very important.

Another way is to integrate specific learning methods such as those first developed in Eastern Europe back in the 1950's.

# What are the Learning Levels?

NLP helps us track our learning by spelling out five levels of learning.

**Subconscious incompetence** means that the person is not only lacking competence in the skill or subject, but they don't even realize that it's an issue. This is the clue-free zone of learning.

**Conscious incompetence** means that the person is aware of the issue and can become motivated to learn.

**Conscious competence** happens as the person develops the skills and is able to use them.

**Subconscious competence** sounds odd. Why would you want to become subconscious? Well, you've heard people say they can do something in their sleep. What they really mean is that the skill has become so much of a set of reflexes or habits, that they do not require a lot of conscious thought. The beauty of that is that they have made room in their brains for more learning. Brain scans show us that the brain is a pattern-recognition tool. Once it learns the pattern and can translate it into a reflex that can be fired off, it moves the pattern into a lower brain center, freeing the higher brain areas to actively get skills that are even more sophisticated to layer on top of that earlier learning. And you know what you get when you add sophisticated skills to largely subconscious skills: **mastery**.

At the level of **mastery**, the person does more than create excellent results; they are creative and flexible; they can respond to new conditions and improvise. They have extra brainpower left over to come up with innovative and adaptive strategies. A master is the one that people turn to for inspiration and training.

Mastery has also been called conscious mastery of subconscious mastery. This means that you are able to gain more conscious access to material, that for most people is not conscious. This is like expanding your intelligence into a larger landscape, or a bigger brain.

Artists do this when they learn to trust their creativity or their muse, accepting signals from their subconscious and trusting those signals to lead them through a productive creative process. Intuition is also like this, because the person has learned how to trust their subconscious to guide them in sizing things up and making good decisions.

Do you see how these phases of learning can guide you in sequencing your learning, and in figuring out where your needs are? Think of a skill you are building, maybe NLP, and see where you are in these phases. Then ask, "What do I most need at this phase?"

# So where do I start?

You start with your identity as a learner. NLP is very aware of something called feedback, and about taking a meta view. For example, teachers who don't have a meta view or who don't pay attention to feedback have two big problems, or maybe I should say, their students have two big problems. Without attention to feedback, the teacher just teaches according to whatever system they learned. Then the response of the student is not as important to the teacher as it should be.

If anything, the teacher may just write off the student's difficulties as them not trying hard enough or just being difficult. The teacher may even feel that emotional abuse is justified. We prefer to believe that this really means that the lessons do not fit the student.

The other big problem is that, without a meta view, the teacher is caught up in the content of the lesson at the expense of other learning resources. One powerful resource is identity; the identity or, you could say, the persons of the educator and the students. When we look at how to use identity as a learning resource, we are coming from a meta view. Take, for example, a simple matter of wording. If you are "wrong", that sounds like it is about who you are.

But if you answered wrongly, it is a dynamic process that can change. It's very nice to see what can happen when you take the word "is" out of some statements.

A teacher found that his students reacted quite

differently to those two wordings. Isn't it something that there is only a difference of two letters between wrong and wrongly?

If two letters can make a difference, imagine what you can do with a rich and positive identity as a learner, free from the emotional abuse and inflexibility of a learning system that makes you wrong?

In fact, it is estimated that most children are not well-suited for the methods used by public education in the United States. What a shame that many teachers are not living up to their potential. If only they would try harder.

Oops! Did you catch what I just said? Doesn't this sound like what they say about kids that don't fit the way the school teaches? It's kind of fun to turn the tables, but consider a better way to look at this. We would want to know how to get teachers excited about this meta view, but from the point of view of the teacher. Well, guess what, NLP has already done this with many teachers. It has already transformed many classrooms through NLP training and books.

Now what about your identity as a learner? I'll bet that you can find some ways studying, practicing and learning have become negatives in your learning identity.

When you associate something like studying with a limited, negative idea, then NLP says you have nominalized it. A nominalization turns a larger reality in to a few limiting things. This is so automatic, that you may not even realize that you have developed this habit. So take a look at learning.

Take a look at you as a person who learns. What images, feelings and judgments flash through your mind?

As we cover more NLP techniques, you will be able to transform things that now seem tedious, tinged with failure, or too challenging into much happier and more effective experiences. You can break the old associations, and replace them with associations that expand you; associations that shift your experience from fear of failure to a desirable challenge.

# How NLP analyses mind and behavior to produce results

NLP is about creating excellence. We can understand how people create excellence, and we can create excellence in ourselves with NLP.

One of the most powerful tools for creating excellence is the representational system, or a rep system for short. The rep system is like a microscope or CAT scan that shows us what is going on inside a person. When we discover powerful methods of excellence, and when we understand how someone is self-sabotaging, we can help them achieve dreams that they felt they would never attain.

# What is a Representational System?

A rep system is how we perceive what comes in through our senses. We may see it, hear it, taste it, feel it, or even smell it. Whatever it is, we call it INFORMATION. The reason we call it information is that your brain interprets and uses it. If breakfast is burning, your first warning is the smell. The smell is information.

The beauty of rep systems is that they go way beyond how things get into your brain. You can recall and think about your experiences, and create new ones, with the power of your mind.

Much of the power of NLP comes from your ability to work with rep systems. Another phrase for rep system is sense modality.

# Well, then, what good are these Rep Systems?

You can use rep systems to really change how you and other people react to situations. With an understanding of rep systems you can even create new techniques, because rep systems help you analyze the strategies of excellent people.

You can look at each of their rep systems and see what is going on. Sometimes this is all it takes to create a system for excellence that you can use or teach.

# What ARE the Rep Systems?

The rep systems include the obvious ones: the five senses. Here are the three main ones. They are what we see (called the visual rep system), what we hear (called the auditory rep system), what we feel (called the kinesthetic rep system). The other two obvious ones may be needed at times. They are what we taste (the gustatory rep system), and what we smell (the olfactory rep system).

Those are the obvious rep systems: the five senses. But there are two factors that give rep systems great value in understanding and achieving excellence. The first is how we talk to ourselves, or hear what others have said. We call this the auditory digital rep system. Changing the talk inside our minds is a very powerful tool.

The other valuable factor is to know which rep system a person favors. That is, which rep system do they rely upon most of the time. This is called the preferred rep system. Once you know what their referred rep system is, you can make a better connection by using that rep system more. You can also make more powerful tools, because that rep system is more powerful for that person.

# It might be interesting to a student, but what makes this so valuable to me?

Rep systems are valuable because they are the way our experiences are coded. They are the DNA of our thoughts and behavior. They are where it all comes from. We encode or absorb our experiences and ideas with rep systems. We call up this information through our rep systems. This is called accessing or retrieving the information.

It isn't always obvious. Ask someone how they know something or why they did something, and they will give you a pretty limited answer. Most people will tell you that they just "know" something, or "felt" like it.

But advertisers don't spend millions of dollars figuring out exactly which sounds and images to put into a television commercial just for the fun of it. And manufacturers don't spend millions on designing just the right shape, color, and smells of products and logos for their egos.

It's all about representational systems, and how they are loaded with meaning and motivation. By decoding the rep systems of successful people, you can get access to secrets that have taken many years or generations to acquire. By decoding the rep systems of someone who is failing, you can become much more valuable as a success resource.

Do you remember when we talked about strategies? The way a person sequences and selects rep systems is a strategy. There is a rep system strategy for everything we do. By becoming aware of this, we gain extraordinary flexibility and latitude for creating better strategies.

One reason for this is that rep systems are so basic, that they afford us great leverage to influence the resulting behaviors AND the results in our lives. Later in the book, we will learn to work with our rep systems in ways that can greatly improve our happiness, and even help resolve serious emotional problems.

# How do I know what Rep System is being used?

The place to start is to learn what rep system the person is relying on the most at any point in time. You can use this rep system to have more influence and connection with the person.

People will tell you what rep system they are using without even knowing it. The secret is in their words. If they talk about how things look, what they saw, colors, and other visual words, they are thinking in pictures quite a bit. They are mostly using their visual rep system. So that is their preferred rep system.

If they talk about what they hear, how things sound,

how loud they are, and other auditory words, they are emphasizing their auditory system.

It is the same thing for feelings. If they sense that someone is dishonest, and have a gut feeling about what stock to buy, they are mostly accessing feelings. That is, they are in their kinesthetic rep system.

Years ago in the U.S., a conservative politician named Barry Goldwater used a kinesthetic phrase in his advertising: "In your heart, you know he's right." That's pretty funny, because by the time he was campaigning, everybody knew that your heart pumps blood, and your brain knows things. But when people have strong feelings about something, they think they know it. This fact has been used by politicians throughout history.

But Goldwater lost his 1964 bid for the presidency of the U.S., because the liberals used even more powerful feelings and images involving fear of nuclear weapons and grief over the Kennedy assassination.

When Hitler was creating his speeches, he spent a good deal of time learning what got the crowds really excited. Of course, we'd like you to use rep systems to do good things, not to invade sovereign nations and sport a bad haircut.

Now, here is something fun and valuable that you can start doing to learn about rep systems. Whenever someone tells you about something, notice which rep system they use the most.

# What Do I do with a Primary Rep System?

Let's say you want to sell me a vacation package. Listen to this, and ask yourself what rep system I'm using. "I just don't SEE how I can afford to take a vacation."

You heard the word see, as in visual. I can't SEE how I'll afford it. Most people use the visual rep system more than the other two main ones, hearing and feeling. This tells you that you must create pictures in my head of your wonderful vacation package. You know that pictures will especially help to influence me.

But consider the internal aspect of seeing. I can't see it because my concern about finances won't let me see it. So when you talk financing, that is the most important point for the visual rep system.

Show me how I'm locking in value while the cost will increase for everyone else. Show me a graph. Show me big, simple numbers. Make me see other people missing out and being jealous of me. Before long, I could be seeing a whole new opportunity.

Now let's say my wife is there, and she has a great influence over my buying decisions, or maybe total influence. Listen for her rep system. "Honey, I'm UNCOMFORTABLE with us committing to something when your work is so FEAST or FAMINE." This wife of mine is all about feelings. No wonder she lights up the room. Uncomfortable, feast, famine... When you're coming up with things to influence her with, you'd better touch her feelings.

She needs to think about how she'll feel finally having some quality time with her feast or famine husband. On our vacation, she can look forward to sunshine, warm sand, and the plush beds and carpeting of the air-conditioned resort.

Did you notice which of those things were not from an external sense? Warm sand affects your senses through your feet. But where does the feeling of quality alone time come from?

**Inside!**

Hey, remember feast or famine. You'd better tell her about the amazing food.

This is a huge lesson for influencing with rep systems. You should appeal to the internal sources as well as external. In fact, the internal sources may be many times more powerful than the external ones. This is because they are often about motivations and values.

NLP uses the term predicate for the clue words that tell you what rep system someone is using. Predicates, as you have seen, are words like see, hear, and feel. Predicates are not always so obvious, though. If I tell you I'm CERTAIN, I might be in the auditory digital mode. That's the one where my internal talk is very dominant.

But what if I not only tell you I'm so CERTAIN, but I also gesture forcefully with my fist. In that case, I'm telling you I FEEL strongly about it. Instead of knowing

I'm right in my head, I know it in my heart; I FEEL it, and I want you to FEEL it, too. Are you with me, or against me? Feelings make choices very simple. So they can make your job simple.

So there's another important tip. Body language can be very important. If someone cocks their head and looks kind of skeptical, that's a sign that they aren't hearing things that they can agree with. They may be taking apart what you said in their own heads, because you weren't being analytical or logical enough for them.

In that case, you need to build more trust so they can get into the feelings or images, or you need to offer up your most compelling evidence, that is, the facts that show that you are right. And keep working on building that trust. You don't need to drop the other sense modalities, but you need to deliver the facts. And did I mention building trust? We'll teach you a lot about rapport-building soon.

But here is a trust-building technique you can start using right away. It's called matching predicates. As you talk to people, practice using the same rep system that they are. See how this affects how they act toward you.

Are they more open to your ideas? Do they show you friendlier body language?

Do they smile more or give you a softer, kinder facial expression?

Since body language is a non-verbal predicate, see what body language you can use that goes along with the rep system you are emphasizing. If they are hearing, cock your head, put your finger to your ear, lean forward a little bit with an ear turned a little toward them.

If they are seeing, tilt your head up just a little and raise your eyebrows a bit, soften your eyes, like you're letting them in.

If they are feeling, use more emotional gestures. Nothing too dramatic for now, just enough to show where your heart is, or at least where it is supposed to be.

Keep in mind that people may change their primary rep system depending on the subject, or even the point of the conversation they are in. So don't think people have only one rep system. Be flexible and follow them into different rep systems.

Also, it's good to appeal to all rep systems during your discussion. In psychology, there is a thing called neurological recruitment. This big phrase means that the more brain cells you can get to think about something, the more powerful it is.

If you're in an airplane, you want ALL the engines firing. Using more rep systems means you are influencing with more power. Emphasize one at a time, but use all of the three primary ones: seeing, feeling, and hearing.

# What else can tell me about a person's Rep Systems?

Another valuable method is to watch for eye movements. These are called eye accessing cues. We call them accessing cues, because the eye movements tell you what senses the person is accessing, or tapping into, in order to think and express themselves.

People have claimed that the research does not support NLP's use of eye accessing cues, but the research has some serious flaws. We suggest that you see for yourself. And remember, this is not always true for every person. We'll talk about the exceptions to the typical eye accessing cues soon.

# What are the common Eye Accessing Cues?

Let's cover the most typical eye accessing cues now. Here is what to watch for. When a person glances up and to the left (your left, their right), they are constructing a visual image. That may mean they are considering something new, or trying out an image that you are creating for them.

So constructing means what it says, the mind is

constructing or creating a more or less new image that they have not seen before. But if they look up and to the left (their left, your right), they are recalling something visual; something they actually remember.

When they look simply to their right, your left, mid range or lateral, they are constructing something auditory; something they have not exactly heard before, or, more likely, a combination or sequence of sounds that they have not heard before. When they look to the left, your right, they are recalling an auditory experience. They are remembering a sound or sound pattern.

When someone looks down and right (your left), they are connecting with a feeling of some kind. But down and to their left (your right), is for digital auditory access; that is, for some kind of verbal information.

As you'll recall, that could be something they are putting together, or something they have already heard. Sound in general, and sound as human speech are two different things to access, so they have different eye movements.

To review, as if you're **facing** them, and see their eyes going:

- Up left is visual constructing.
- Up right is visual recalled.
- Directly / laterally left is auditory constructing.
- Directly / laterally right is auditory recall.
- Down left is kinesthetic.
- Down right is verbal memory or self talk.

You might want to draw a diagram of that, or use the one we offer on our website, NLPWeeklyMagazine.com.

Practice watching people on television to see what they do with their eyes.

It can be complicated sometimes, because people may access a sequence of different kinds of representations rather quickly. A common pattern is to access a memory and then look down and to the right to decide what to say about it.

These eye accessing cues can give you advance notice of what rep systems a person is relying on. To improve your connection and persuasiveness, you can use them to match up with their rep system as well.

# But is everybody wired like this?

There are some people whose eye accessing cues are reversed. NLP theorists believe that they tend to be left-handed and have their brain hemisphere functions on opposite sides from most people.

There are even some people whose eye movements are very slight, very subtle. You have to look more carefully to see what their eyes are doing.

This means that you need to observe and see what their eye movements indicate. If they don't match what I've told you, first see if they are reversed.

If their eye movements seem more mixed or random, there may be some reason, such as a neurological problem or agitation.

You may even notice that there is a direction that their eyes never go. This may be a rep system that is off-limits for some reason. It is a good idea to avoid using predicates for that rep system!

If the person always starts off with a particular direction, before making other moves, this is called their lead rep system. They access one particular rep system so they can get started, then move on to other rep systems. This lead system is not necessarily their primary rep system. It's just the rep system they access to get started.

# What are Submodalities?

Another word for a rep system is a modality. You could say that submodalities are the building blocks of each sense modality / representational system. For example, imagine looking at a tree. Thank you. Now how clear or fuzzy was the image? How bright or dark? How colorful was it?

Since I asked you to look at the tree, we were using the visual rep system. The submodalities were clarity, brightness and color saturation.

Let's try it with the auditory rep system. Imagine listening to the birds in the tree.

- How loud did the birds sound to you?
- How clear was the sound?
- Were they high pitched?
- Was the sound soothing?

In a way, you can use the same submodality to analyze more than one representational system. When someone says colors are loud, they don't mean that the colors make a sound, they mean they are more dominating and bright, maybe too much so.

When someone says a sound is sharp, they don't mean you can cut with it, they mean it's edgy, maybe even irritating.

When someone says they feel blue, they don't mean their skin is turning blue. They mean they are sad or maybe depressed.

Let's do some kinesthetic submodalities. How do you feel about looking at the tree and listening to the birds? It is relaxing? Are you uncomfortable, because the exercise feels like work? Is it uplifting? Notice that we have made a really big change here.

I could have asked you to imagine a breeze touching your skin, but instead, I asked for your internal reaction to the tree and birds. Both are kinesthetic, but this time we went for something that springs from you rather than touches you directly.

When you tune into your emotions and your body, you notice things like a nerve center firing off feelings, or tension, or relaxation, or blushing. Together, these and many other sensations blend into an emotion, like attraction, feeling like dancing, romance, sexual arousal, or stress; but hopefully without the stress.

# What is the difference between Digital and Analogue Submodalities?

Remember when we talked about the eye accessing cue that went in the auditory digital direction? We were talking about what happens when people not only hear a sound, but that sound is words. When a submodality is digital, what we really mean is that it contains information expressed using known symbols. You can take words that you have heard, and write them. Now they are visual.

Put them in Braille. Now they are kinesthetic, if you know Braille, anyway. Put them on a giant billboard in Times Square, and you have added the size submodality. Light them up and you have added the brightness submodality.

All those other submodalities were analogue. In other words, you can scale them up or down or in some other way, and they are still the same basic sound, sight or feeling. But if you take that billboard and add a bunch of letters to it, the digital message will not be the same. Make a red light brighter, it's still a red light. Add fifty letters at random to your marketing slogan, and it doesn't mean anything anymore. It's easy to break a digital modality. But you can scale analog modalities a lot before you can no longer perceive them effectively. For example, you'd have to make a color so bright that it is blinding, or so dark that it is invisible.

It is important to choose the right digital submodality. For example, we don't recommend tasting Morse code. It would be very slow to get a message from caramel, strawberry... strawberry, caramel, strawberry, strawberry... Strawberry, caramel, caramel, strawberry. That was NLP in Morse code, and it was slow just saying the flavors, much less tasting them. I suppose it could be fun, though, even if you don't know Morse code.

# Give me an example. What can I do with Submodalities?

We'll start with something basic. Think of something that you were supposed to do, but didn't really want to, because it was too tedious, like a lot of paper work, or too intimidating, like talking to a boss about a mistake. Something that you still haven't finished. Think of the last time you tried to do it. See yourself at the desk, or talking to the person, whatever the situation was.

What images make up this memory? What do you see? ... And what do you hear? ... What do you feel? ...

I'm going to mention some submodalities that might be the ones making things unpleasant. Is the image too overpowering, so that it bothers you, or is it to small, dark, or vague, so you have trouble finding your way? ... Do you hear negative talk about you from someone or from yourself? ... Do you feel tension, or a bad feeling in your gut that makes you want to avoid the situation or not prepare for it somehow?

Analyze this memory a little more, and see what modalities and then what submodalities bring the real discomfort and avoidance...

We'll come back to this memory later, and we'll do something with it to help you with this situation even more.

Now recall a very pleasant memory, anything that makes you feel good. Maybe relaxing in a park with a friend, or listening to a concert, or taking a hike. Anything that comes to mind... Notice how it makes you feel. You know it's a pleasant memory, because it is pleasant to remember.

Which modality is strongest in creating that good feeling? Is seeing or hearing giving you the strongest good feeling? If the situation is very beautiful, or you realize the person's voice or the concert are wonderful sounds, then you know which sensory modality is driving the feeling...

Now pay attention to the feeling that comes from this memory. Where in your body is most of the feeling? ... Does the feeling move in any way? Does it seem to flow, wash, or press in any direction? ... Does the feeling have any vibration, maybe just a very gentle vibration or tingling? ...

There is a reason we have good feeling words like inspiration, uplifting, expansive, soaring, or titillating. They express submodalities. If a good feeling swells up from your chest, then the submodality is movement, and probably some others as well.

If you feel motivated to have another experience like that, you could discover that there are a lot of submodality feelings that make up that one feeling you call motivations. And that's just feelings. There are submodalities that make up your ideas and expectations as well.

As you can tell, this is a very deep subject. The more you work with rep systems, the more you will find that it comes naturally to you. The results you can get from working with them are very gratifying.

# What is Mapping Across?

Mapping across means that you take resources from one state into another one. Robert Dilts' research into meta-programs helped us figure out how to do this. Mapping across changes the meta-program, and creates different results.

For example, lets say that you supervise someone who gets into a bad mood every time a customer talks to him in a certain tone of voice. The employee has trouble making the customer happy, and sometimes even upsets certain customers. This is bad for business, and the employee is spending a lot of time feeling unhappy.

This employee has had very good experiences with people. Pretty much everyone has. This means the employee has resources he can use to change his behavior. In one state, he feels good about people. In the other state, he feels bad, and acts badly, too. Mapping across means you use the good state to change the bad one. You get the resources from that good state to map across to the situations that normally bring out the bad state. Once you have mapped across, the employee will have an easy time responding to customers that have an attitude. He'll even enjoy having more self-mastery, happiness, and job security.

# How do you map across? What is the Swish Pattern?

The swish pattern is a popular way to map across. Let's use that situation of yours in which you did not want to do something, when we were learning about submodalities. As you recall, you had certain submodalities driving a bad feeling that made it hard to do something.

First, imagine yourself in a great state of mind, enjoying the benefit of doing what you didn't want to do.

That could be having a vacation, buying something, your boss shaking your hand, mailing your taxes in and being happy that you finished this.

Imagine something good that you get to do, because you took care of the situation.

What submodalities make this a happy or positive image? Imagine that you can make them bigger, brighter, louder, or anything else that adds impact and makes you feel better. It's like turning a dial to adjust volume of a music player. Expand the image so it seems to fill your entire field of vision.

Now imagine that you can place that image in one of your hands. Whichever hand feels happier at the moment. The image is in the palm of your hand.

Now draw your hand back away from your face. Place the image that you started with, having trouble with the situation, in the other hand.

The problem image is in that other hand. Hold it up to your face, as if you are looking closely at the negative image in your hand.

Now prepare for a sudden switch of hand positions. The negative image will shoot back while the other hand will bring the positive image up to your face. Yell, "Swish!" when you do it. Ready? Go! "Swish!"

Now make sure you are really connecting with the positive image and all the good feelings connected with it - confidence, satisfaction, whatever.

Do this a few more times, until the transition feels

very fast and complete. Later today and tomorrow do this swishing at least two more times. Now see how you feel the next time you are in the situation.

When the swish pattern works, it becomes easy to be in the right state of mind for the situation. This pattern can be used for many different problems.

There are various ways to do the swish pattern. For example, if you want to practice in a library, you can pretend the positive image is pulled back on a tight rubber band. When you let it go, it snaps through the negative image. That way you don't have to make gestures or yell.

# What is the Godiva Chocolate Pattern?

This is another exercise in submodality power. Many people use it to improve motivation or develop other valuable feelings. Try this one for some chore that you don't enjoy doing, like cleaning or budgeting. The Godiva Chocolate pattern is a way to feed good feelings and motivation directly into a task that you currently find disagreeable. The idea is to give you a compulsive desire to do this, and lose the bad feelings about it.

Start with an image of something that you ALREADY intensely desire and feel compelled to indulge in. Perhaps there is a chocolate treat that you favor. Amplify the submodalities that make it desirable. See how well you can stir up excitement, happiness, and desire with this image.

Next, imagine seeing yourself doing the task that you WANT to want to do. You know what I mean? The task that you SHOULD want to do.

Now, do what we call an ecology check: If any part of you objects to this task becoming a desire of yours, speak up now. If you have any objections, see if there is a better way to achieve your higher objective, or choose a different task for this process.

Now imagine the picture of what you are supposed to do right there before you. You are watching yourself do the task. The picture of your desire is right behind it, where you can't see it.

Now imagine a hole opening quickly in the picture, so that you can get a good view of your desire when you look through the hole. Enjoy whatever happy feelings come from this view. Really emphasize the joy of this image.

Now allow the hole to close, but slow enough that you can maintain that nice feeling while you again gaze at the task picture. See what it's like to harbor that happy, desiring feeling while you look at the task picture.

Do that opening and closing again a few more times. You are connecting good feelings and desire with the task.

Once you're done, see how it feels to bring up the task in your mind. Now we'll see if it really becomes easier to do the task. As they say, the proof is in the pudding (or the chocolate).

# This is great! What could possibly go wrong?

Even people who pride themselves on their common sense may launch into a behavior change that their subconscious mind would want to sabotage. For this reason, it is very important to know that you are making changes that can stick and that don't cause other problems. We call this checking the ecology.

In other words, will the new behavior work out well in other situations, and will it get along well with your other motivations? Doing an ecological check prior to using NLP techniques is usually a good idea. It can challenge you to come up with a better solution.

# What are the NLP Presuppositions?

The NLP presuppositions are the most important guidelines for learning and doing NLP, and for being successful in life. Some people have published a larger number than we have here and some have published less. We feel that this is the best, most useful collection. The word presupposition means something that you may not be able to prove, but that you base your behavior on. As a thinking person, you can see if there are exceptions to these rules, or situations where they don't apply.

## 1. "The 'map' is not the 'territory'" ("the menu is not the meal").

We base our actions on our mental map of the world. If you understand this, you understand that there are always ways to improve your map.

People who are stuck in life don't know this. They get angry or passive when you talk about improving their view of the world. Can you see how knowing that the map is not the territory can make you more flexible and adaptable?

As in evolution, flexibility and adaptability are powerful traits for survival and satisfaction.

## 2. People respond according to their internal maps.

If you don't understand someone, you don't understand his / her mental map. You may understand what they should do, but you can only understand their internal map by learning about it.

Can you imagine what kind of connection you will be able to make with people, and how much better you will react to people when you have all the curiosity and tools that come from this point of view?

## 3. Meaning operates context-dependently.

If you really want to understand what something means to someone, you have to understand the situation, that is, the context. Context has many sides to it. You must understand a politician's motives to understand the real meaning of their speech. You must understand what a person has gone through in order to understand why they are reacting strongly to someone they hardly know. If someone in an artist commune says they love you, it may mean something different than an "I love you" from your aunt. Think of the ways you can expand your view of the world and your understanding of human behavior by delving into context.

### 4. Mind-and-body affect each other.

We are not brains in jars, like in some science fiction movie. We don't just think with our brains, we think with our bodies. Science is revealing more about this all the time. Successful leaders, sales people and others intuitively understand this.

Can you think of some ways you can use this knowledge to your advantage?

Some of the basic applications of this are the value of eating the right food and getting good physical exercise. These have a great impact on your mind.

If you are trying to have a talk with an uncooperative teenager, see how they act if you take a walk with them. More advanced use of this know-how lies in fields such as body mind, or somatic-psychotherapy, participatory learning methods, and the use of evolutionary psychology in marketing, where primitive drives and instincts are brought into play.

## 5. Individual skills function by developing and sequencing rep systems.

You have already gotten a taste of this powerful knowledge. The submodality techniques we tried are used to create many kinds of behavior change and success. Imagine what your life would be like if you applied one or more tools from a rich toolbox full of such methods every day?

What experts or successful person would you most like to model using this insight?

## 6. We respect each person's model of the world.

You may not agree with everyone, but if you respect their model of the world, you can understand it and find ways to create more understanding, less conflict, and more good outcomes.

Think of some of the people that you have reacted to too quickly or too harshly. People that you judged. Some of those situations caused you to lose opportunities.

Imagine what genuine interest and concern for people's models of the world can do for you in a world that is very diverse, political, and charged with sensitive issues? You can become a great navigator, and fare better than many people who are quite smart, but fail to understand this wisdom.

## 7. Person and behavior describe different phenomena. We "are" more than our behavior.

The idea that we are more than our behavior is a very profound idea. You could write many volumes about this from your own life once you unlock this insight.

Let's just look at how deeply people are able to change, and why they change. Most people are on the verge of a very expanded way of being in the world, and don't even know it.

We have no idea what any person's true potential or destiny is. Whenever someone tells someone else that they will not amount to anything, that person is failing to understand the truth of this proposition; the truth that we are more than our behavior. In many places, a pattern of behavior or even a single act can define you.

The idea of a human birth right, or inalienable rights that many constitutional governments are charged with supporting is really a profound philosophical position that NLP expresses as well.

Whatever you have done wrong, learn from it; don't let it define you. Whatever your limitations are, get clear on how to move forward in harmony with your abilities and limits, don't just use will power to try harder, or sentence yourself to a life of shame.

You are bigger than that, whether you know it or not. Imagine the talent and energy that can be liberated in the world as this idea becomes better understood and more widely expressed.

## 8. Every behavior has utility and usefulness—in some context.

This idea can be very counter-intuitive. There are many behaviors that seem to make no sense, and are simply irritating and inconvenient at best, or criminal and threatening at worst. Milton Erickson, the famous psychiatrist and hypnotherapist that NLP has studied was a great model for this wisdom.

He did something called utilization. Often it involved finding the hidden power or motivation within the behavior that was the easiest to try to stop or ignore.

Do you know someone who does something that troubles you or otherwise seems to be a problem?

Think about ways that the behavior might be used to support some kind of change, or how it may reveal motivations that you could somehow connect with a more effective behavior. You can even take this approach with yourself.

What kind of potential might you release by having an attitude like that about yourself?

## 9. We evaluate behavior & change in terms of context and ecology.

NLP has been influenced by a very important approach called systems theory. The basic idea of systems theory is that we must consider how the parts of the world interact with each other. When you make a change in one part, how does this cause a domino effect?

Systems theory applies to the human body, to families, organizations, ecology, nations, and the world. We could never do justice to systems theory in this book, but we will share this with you.

Consider the systems impact or, as we say, the ecological impact of any change you consider, or of any behavior you want to understand. It is an added dimension to behavior that gives you a larger and more interesting world, and gives you much more power for making change. It can also help to protect you from unexpected reactions from a system.

### 10. We cannot not communicate.

So true! Your clothes, your accent, your body language, the subtle expressions that flit across your face, - all communicate; all signal things to the people around you. We all size each other up all the time.

If someone tells you never to judge people, perhaps they mean not to limit that person or to be harsh, but you can't stop interpreting other's behavior and signals.

You do this from the most primitive parts of your brain that have radar for danger, to your more sophisticated abilities to determine who can offer the best relationships to you. This is an important reason for NLP to exist.

The more you can align your subconscious and conscious motives, the more your subtle behaviors will communicate the right message. One of the biggest ingredients for charisma is this alignment, or coherence.

## 11. The way we communicate affects perception & reception.

You don't just communicate a digital message. You send out your own collection of submodalities that affect how you are perceived, and even others' ability to perceive you accurately.

If you use conservative language to express liberal ideas or vice versa, peoples' filters will screen out the content of your message and just hear that you are conservative or liberal, unless they are very analytical types, and those are in the minority.

Even the analytical types will probably feel uncomfortable with you, despite hearing what you were actually saying. They will only be comfortable if they are in on the joke. As a communicator, part of your job is to know about your listeners' filters.

What are the keys that will open their minds to what you have to say?

The valuable lessons of NLP on creating rapport are a great contribution to this quest.

## 12. The meaning of communication lies in the response you get.

This is one of the most fundamental and early lessons to get from your study of NLP. Regardless of what you intended to say, the communication is what the other person heard.

By carefully observing the other person's response, you can determine whether you have communicated effectively.

People who fail to take responsibility for this fail to communicate effectively. You could say that they don't care if they are broadcasting on the wrong station and nobody is hearing them.

Of course, you will not be able to do this if the person is purposely misunderstanding you.

That is a tactic that some people use when they want to cast doubt on what you are saying or manipulate you. But as a sensitive communicator, you will learn to tell the difference, and develop creative responses to that kind of thing. NLP is a wonderful art to help you deal with manipulative people.

## 13. The one who sets the frame for the communication controls the action.

Like our brains, communication doesn't exist in a vacuum. You can exert much more influence when you understand the frame around a communication. The frame consists of things like the assumptions about why the discussion is taking place, what the environment means about it, that sort of thing.

The presuppositions we're covering here set the stage for NLP. Every communication comes in a package of presuppositions.

Presuppositions can be constructive when they provide

positive guidance. But they can cause harm, as they do when they serve to filter and bias propaganda. Instead of being a sitting duck, you can be proactive.

Before an important discussion, ask yourself what the frame will be if you do nothing. Consider how it may support or defeat your objectives. Then think about how that frame might be improved.

### 14. "There is no failure, only feedback."

This is a philosophy, not a scientific fact. As a philosophy, it is something you can live by. If you turn your failures into learning experiences, you gain so many benefits; we can't list them all here. But consider these: Instead of losing sleep and feeling ashamed, you will be inspired and focused; you will build confidence as you learn from your experiences.

Instead of procrastinating and getting caught up in trivial matters, you will act on what is truly important to you. Why? Because you will not fear failure. When postponing your destiny becomes more uncomfortable than the risks you take in pursuing success, then you are ready to live this philosophy.

### 15. The person with the most flexibility exercises the most influence in the system.

We have all seen the way inflexible people can only function in a certain culture or lifestyle. Take them out of their element, and they cannot adapt.

Well, life is about change. That means that you will need flexibility in order to adapt to change. Since you can depend on change, you must depend on your adaptive creativity. NLP stresses the importance of meta level thinking. That is, looking at the situation from a higher level, not being caught up in the obvious.

From a meta level, you can see how things are changing, and you can free yourself from rigid roles and seize upon opportunities that are invisible to everyone else. A good place to start is to ask yourself who you think you are, maybe in terms of your career. Then ask how that self-definition may be limiting you.

Ask yourself how your world or your career field is changing and creating opportunities that adaptable people can benefit from.

### 16. Resistance indicates the lack of rapport.

This is especially important for sales people, consultants, coaches and psychotherapists. If your customer is resisting doing what is best, don't get mad; get rapport. As soon as you start seeing the person as resistant, you have locked onto your agenda and become inflexible. Remember what we just said about flexibility.

This is a perfect example. Not only do you want to use the NLP rapport-building skills in general, but in situations with resistance - you need to better understand their motives, their values, and their ecology.

Resistance often comes because the change you want

to see would conflict with something you don't even know about.

This is why sales people qualify their customers. Part of qualifying a customer is to ask them how a product or service would or would not work in their lives.

Often, people are resisting what they THINK you are trying to do, rather than what you ARE trying to do. This takes us back to the importance of framing. If someone is quick to misjudge you, this is part of the frame.

One critical way to prevent or cure this kind of bad frame is rapport. Erase resistance from your vocabulary and focus on what is driving the person and on gaining rapport with them.

## 17. People have the internal resources they need to succeed.

This belief generates excellence, because when you believe in people's internal resources, you believe in your clients and your respect your competitors. This is a very powerful position. With clients, one will dig deeper to find the creativity and doggedness that they need in order to become a master consultant or coach. With yourself, you will never give up.

If you do not succeed, you will not collapse into failure, you will call upon your creativity. This kind of creativity is the force that brings out your hidden resources. One of the greatest things about NLP is that is can help you surprise yourself in wonderful way.

## 18. Humans have the ability to experience one-trial learning.

You have seen people fail to learn the same life lesson over and over again. Perhaps you've seen them date or marry the wrong person time and again.

People do this because they have not liberated the kind of insight and creativity that the NLP presuppositions encourage. Living with a meta level view, living in a truly awake state, and living with inspiring objectives before you give you too much momentum to fall into the same hole over and over again.

Ask yourself about a negative life experience that you have had more than once.

With that in mind, review the NLP presuppositions and I guarantee you, you will find several that can come to your aid. Failure is extinct when you liberate your learning potential.


## 19. All communication should increase choice.

When you pay attention to the frame of communication, and when you develop the learning and flexibility that NLP teaches, you become a master communicator. You develop the ability to expand choices.

Hidden frames limit choices. Rigidity limits choices. Failing to see people's inner resources limit choices. All of the presuppositions in some way expand the range of choices.

By infusing your communication with the lessons of NLP, you can expand your own and others' choices. Listen carefully to the next conversation you overhear. There are probably various ways that one or both parties are limiting their choices.

- Ask yourself what you detect in that conversation that limits choice?
- How can you have a conversation like that differently?
- How can you knock down barriers to choice when you communicate?

## 20. People make the best choices open to them when they act.

Never take for granted that other people know what you know. They may have all the options that you have, but they don't know it. People make bad choices and limit themselves because they have not connected to the inner resources that will liberate them.

This applies to people who end up in jail, in dead-end careers, and in endless arguments. Don't get mad at them, especially if you are a supervisor or coach. Often, very simple and direct instruction and training is all that is needed.

Other times, the person needs to get involved in something more psychological, like working with a successful NLP practitioner.

**21. As response-able persons, we can run our own brain and control our results.**

This is the most fundamental discovery that people make as they become truly conscious. Waking up to this choice gives you an entirely different fate. You have heard people who sound like juvenile delinquents, when they do something wrong, they always have someone to blame. When they are held accountable, everyone is being unfair to them. Well, even mature adults fall into this thinking at times, as they do when they say that someone has made them feel a certain way.

If you have learned to run your own brain, you have better things to do than complain about how someone made you feel. You take that situation as a call to expand your choices; a call to experience a creative, confident, resourceful state when you are dealing with that person and their attitude; a call to know what your objectives really are in that situation.

You need to know what a truly great outcome would be, so that you can bring it about. That is about controlling your results. You may not have a magic wand, but you have something close to a magic wand when you are very clear about your ideal outcomes.

People who lack this are rudderless ships, spending too much time complaining about their bad results and bad feelings. No one needs to live like that. And you are learning many tools and perspectives that can take you light years beyond that existence, and into a far more successful way of being.

# What are Perceptual Positions?

Perceptual positions can really help you with visualization as a tool for excellence.

Perceptual positions are a bit like the persons (i.e. 1st, 2nd and 3rd) in grammar, but, of course, these positions are used in NLP for visualization. Let's take a look at each one.

**The first position** can really help you feel down to earth or grounded. It can help you tune into your own power as a person and feel whole. This first position is seeing the scene through your own eyes. It is called the "fully associated" position, because any other position is disconnected from your normal sensory experiences and your thoughts.

In the first position, your seeing, hearing, and feeling are all where they should be when you are 100% in your body and in touch with your senses.

**The second position** can help you create a more convincing communication strategy. It can help you develop more empathy, understanding people's feelings in a richer way, by walking in the other person's shoes. In the second position, you see and hear yourself through someone else's eyes, and you imagine experiencing their reaction to you.

**The third position** is a great way to see things more

objectively without emotions distracting you. In the third position you see yourself as if you are watching a movie of the whole situation. We have already done a process from the third position. Now you know what to call it. You also see any other people from that more distant position.

You can build inner resources from the third position, and you can analyze what's going on from a cool-headed point of view.

**"How would this conversation or event look to someone totally uninvolved?"**

Imagine yourself being out of your body and off to the side of the conversation between you and the other person. You can see both yourself and the other person. The third position allows you to step back, to gain a sense of distance, to observe, to witness, to feel neutral and to appreciate both positions fully.

**The fourth position** can give you a view of the systems that are involved; systems like the family or organizations that are part of the situation; that are connected with it in some way. The fourth position can help you explore how the situation came to be as it is.

This perspective can open up a new channel of creative solutions for any situation, even for situations that appear to involve only one person. That's because every individual is in a cultural and social reality. Remember the NLP presupposition that every communication derives its meaning from its context. You could say that about every life as well.

In the fourth position, you take on the collective point

of view. It's a little like being the sap flowing through all the branches of a tree; you aren't just looking at the tree. As you look at the situation, try saying things like, "The kind of outcomes that would work for us are..." or "The way we should discuss this is..."

As you can tell, the fourth position is about us; it's about the collective good and the motives that run through the system, whether it's two people or a global corporation.

**The fifth position** can give you a cosmic view that is like being enlightened and beyond the whole situation. This cosmic view comes about because the fifth position is more dissociated that any of other positions.

Sometimes it can be healing simply because it gives you a transcendent perspective that can bring a sense of peace that you have not experienced in that situation. It can permanently change your experience and your reactions to it.

Getting into the fifth position may take some practice, because it is so foreign to most cultures. Experienced meditators, though, may have already been there and will appreciate seeing how it can be used in NLP.

One way to get a sense of the fifth position is to come from the God place. This is where you imagine being the source of what is going on, whether it's an argument, cancer, or a law suit. At the same time, you hold the people involved, including yourself, in pure, loving compassion. Then you beam healing and hope into the situation, where that healing and hope are resources that those involved can absorb as they are ready. If you feel that the universe is a threatening place, or you hate your idea of God, you might appreciate getting a vacation from that state of mind.

# What can I do with Perceptual Positions?

Here is an example of how you can use perceptual positions. Sometimes you need to imagine a situation without a lot of emotion distracting you. When you get out of first position you can get some of that distance. Sometimes the emotional charge can hold a person back. They may feel confused, or intimidated. They are close to a creative solution, but see nothing but desire for revenge. They may need to build confidence, but be limited because someone else's voice is in the foreground of their mind, a voice that attacks their identity and confidence.

But that's just the beginning. I'm going to share with you an easy, but powerful way that the second position can help you generate a positive state; a state that can win you a job, a contract, or a date. By getting into the third position, and imagining how you look in a positive state, you can build and amplify that positive state.

You can try this simple process right now.

Imagine watching a movie of yourself walking to a

meeting where you need a lot of charisma. While you watch yourself walking, feed a lot of golden charisma energy into yourself. Give yourself great posture and a swinging stride. See the energized confidence on your face.

Remember, this is not to cast a magic spell. This is to help you generate a very positive state that is good for meetings and discussions.

Now imagine yourself in that meeting. But keep the sound turned off so that you can concentrate on the image and the state. See yourself really wowing them with your charisma: through your gestures, your face, your body language and everything else. How do you feel doing this? Is it helping you generate a positive state within your real self?

Now see the other people really responding well to everything you do. You can add handshakes, signing of contracts, whatever you like. Take a moment to enjoy the improvements to your state...

# What is the Perceptual Positions Alignment Pattern?

The Perceptual Positions Alignment Pattern takes perceptual positions to another level. Here's what we mean by aligned perceptual positions: it means that all three major rep systems are in the same perceptual position at the same time. This ability allows people to do things with NLP that they were unable to do before they learned it.

While some people get stuck in a perceptual position, most of us get our rep systems split up across more than one perceptual position.

# What happens when Perceptual Positions are not aligned?

Here's a great example. Let's say someone is a bit self-centered or narcissistic. They have trouble tolerating it when someone else has more expensive clothes than they do, or is more important than they are in some way. When they work with perceptual positions, they may find that when they try position number two, which is looking at themselves through the other person's eyes, they discover that what they are hearing is not really the other person's voice. Instead, they hear what seems to be their own voice telling them that they are inferior, that someone else is better than they are.

But they go on to another discovery. Those thoughts add an emotional energy to that judgement. Those thought are loaded with the feeling that it is not acceptable, that it is horrible that this other person has a better car or whatever.

This person has been so busy trying to push away those feelings that they have been preoccupied with gaining status in any way they can. This means they have not realized how they are being driven by a voice that they have lost in the second perceptual position, and that they are being attacked with feelings lost in the second perceptual position.

It gets a little farther out than even that. They realize, doing this work, that the thoughts are not really exactly their own. Those thoughts about inferiority and superiority were the best thing they could come up with when they were a child with a parent who humiliated them and was very harsh. You could say then, that they kind of inherited the voice from the parent; the voice was primarily coming out of second position. That judgmental voice had gotten assigned to random people, but is was not from them, it was from the parent, who was very judgmental.

And the feelings? Those are first position feelings, and that's good, because we are imagining from first position, from inside our own skin. But these intolerable feelings aren't really a reaction to other people having nicer things. Those feelings are the terror of a child who fears the big harsh parent.

It's just that those thoughts and feelings were a defensive or protective posture. Defenses tend to stick around, because they are there to protect us. Unfortunately for this fellow, though, they went out of date long ago. However, he didn't know what they were, so he became lost in a struggle with what they had become.

For him, they had become a drama of who is best, who has the nicest things, who is superior and inferior. The fear of the parent became the fear of anyone being superior. This, in turn, became a struggle for prestige; a struggle that seems like an adult struggle, but is actually a holdover from the past. It's very difficult for someone to untangle themselves from a drama that masquerades as a grown-up pursuit. Aligning perceptual positions can rescue people from such suffering, and it can unlock maturation that has been frozen, maybe for decades.

The beauty of aligning your perceptual positions is that it makes it much easier to let go of feelings and thoughts that don't belong to you. When you are aligned, the misaligned aspects feel out of place. You want to put them where they belong: in the past, or given back to the person who started them in the first place. Many NLP practitioners work without talking about the past. That can work, because alignment happens in the present, and you can let go of thoughts and feelings without knowing where they came from. Most are practical and work with or assess past experience as necessary. They don't, however, get lost in the past; the focus is on outcomes.

# What do aligned Perceptual Positions feel like?

Let me give you a sense of aligned perceptual positions. Imagine yourself listening to this book. As you listen, keep your eyes open, notice that you can see out of your own eyes, feel your own body, and hear with your own ears. You know that each of those senses is yours, because of where you sense them. You are the center and they are in the right positions.

So what we have done is use a real experience with your rep systems that you can refer to when you do visualization or a perceptual position alignment exercise.

# How do I know if my Perceptual Positions are not aligned?

Let's actually imagine something and see if you get the same thing; the same sense of properly placed senses as you did in real life. Let's see if, in a visualization, you are the center of properly placed senses.

First, pick a situation that is challenging for you, and involves another person, like having an argument with someone... Imagine yourself in that challenging situation. First, consider what you are seeing. Is your vision 100% exactly where it would be if you were really there, or would you say it is placed a little off from where it should be? Or do you find yourself looking at yourself? That kind of thing is not aligned with the first perceptual position is it? If vision is not coming from the right place, then it is not coming to you in the way that you experience vision in real life.

Let's try this with hearing. In the imaginary and challenging situation, imagine the sounds you might hear in the situation or add some appropriate sounds... Do they feel that they are coming to you in the same position for real hearing does?

Imagine what the person might say to you... If they are saying what you are thinking, or saying things that are really how YOU feel about yourself, or what YOU feel insecure about, then you are hearing your own thoughts from a different perceptual position. But in the first position, your thoughts should come from where they normally would, not from someone else.

But this can be tricky, especially if you tend to project, that is, if you tend to feel like other people are thinking things ABOUT you that actually come FROM you. If you are very self-conscious, that's probably what's happening, but without you knowing it; it's a subconscious habit.

When people discover this, NLP has just given them a huge gift; the gift of regaining their power in relationships; power that comes from owning their own thoughts. When you are fully aligned, your internal auditory digital, that is, your verbal thoughts, will be placed so that they very much belong to you and help you feel connected and grounded. You can't feel shy or self-conscious in that state, a fully aligned state.

You can do the same thing with feelings.

## Do you have emotions in this challenging situation?

Tension? Nervousness? Any other feelings?

If you are aligned, they are coming from the part of your body that they should come from. But if your kinesthetic rep system is not aligned, then your feelings may seem to be coming from elsewhere. They might be a little off, or way off, like when you project feelings onto someone else.

A more common problem, though, is when people pick up other people's feelings as their own. This makes a person too easy to manipulate. Con artists, addicts, and other destructive people are drawn to these overly empathic individuals. Codependence involves this problem of being at the mercy of other people's feelings.

To sum up, when all your rep systems are in the same perceptual position, you see, hear, and feel your senses in the right physical location. If you are imagining yourself in the first perceptual position, then it is like you are actually in your own body, looking through your own eyes. You feel grounded or connected, even more powerful as an individual.

# How does this work in other perceptual positions?

Other aligned perceptual positions work in pretty much the same way, except from a different point of view. Let's consider the third perceptual position, where you are looking at yourself. Let's use the movie theater again. You're seeing yourself in that challenging situation, while seated in the seat in the movie theater.

When the other person speaks to you in the movie, you don't hear them talking directly to you in your theater seat. Their voice is over near the **you** that is in the movie.

Your vision of the movie as you watch it should be aligned with your eyes as they would be if you're sitting in the theater.

If you are emotional in the movie, you do not feel the emotions, but you might feel empathy. If you are upset in the movie, you might feel sad about it. Audiences feel all sorts of feelings while they watch movies, of course. You might even feel the same kind of feeling, but from your observer point of view.

If you get as angry as your movie self, the anger probably has a little different quality. You might feel something more like wanting to see revenge or wanting to protect your movie self somehow.

This is a very important point, this idea that you can't

feel the feelings of your movie self. If you are truly in third position, you will not feel those exact feelings.

**Can you see how this could be useful for processes in which the person needs some distance from their feelings?**

When a person is not associated into their feelings, they will be less distracted. We use the word "dissociated" for not being associated into your feelings or thoughts. When people experience extreme dissociation, they feel very disconnected. With perceptual positions, you can kind of regulate your amount of dissociation so that it's just right for whatever you're doing.

Now here is an advanced secret. When it comes to challenging situations, very few people find that their perceptual positions are aligned. This is true no matter which perceptual position they explore. This is the secret to the power of perceptual position alignment. Once you align your perceptual position, you will have an edge that is rare for people in challenging situations.

Very often, it is the misalignment itself that is the cause of the challenge in the first place. You could say that once you have aligned perceptual positions, you have drained the swamp so you can see whether there really are any alligators to worry about.

# How do I align my Perceptual Positions?

We call this Perceptual Position Alignment. You start your alignment by finding where the misalignment is. This means you imagine a challenging situation, just as we did above. Then you check each primary perceptual position, seeing, hearing, and feeling. Once we know where the misalignment is, we can use that for the alignment.

So you have already started the process. You discovered whether you had any misalignment in your first perceptual position.

Now you are ready to align the perceptual positions.

### Third Position, Observer

We will start with the observer position, that is, the third perceptual position, because it can be a powerful position to start from and it gives you some dissociation. Sometimes, when you align one perceptual position, others will get aligned on their own.

Let's start with the visual sense.

### Visual:

As you look that your challenging situation, move your point of view out and away, so that you are looking at yourself and the other person.

Now you are in third position. Place your point of view so that you and the other person are both the same distance from your point of view, or observer. Have them be at eye level.

Do you notice any changes, just from doing this perspective change? ...

See if you need to move closer or farther away, to feel like you have a good sense of perspective.

Is there anything else to adjust? Any other submodalities? Is it dark or fuzzy? Make any additional adjustments if you like...

**Auditory:**

How is the auditory? Are you hearing what is going on from where your point of view is? Adjust that as needed to get your hearing into the right position...

And how about any mental comments that are going on? Your mental commentary may be a subtle or emotional one that needs you to find the words. What judgements, fears, or opinions are running through your mind?

Ask yourself if those thoughts are really yours. Do they feel like they are really from your values and from the core of your mind, or are they more like scars or lightning bolts from the edge of your mind, like something that came along for the ride? Or are some of your thoughts actually what you think the other person is thinking?

Remember, as the observer, any thoughts that belong to the other person, or yourself in your imagination, should just be in them, not in your mind as observer. You only know what they are thinking when they say it.

It can be very powerful, when you find yourself distracted by what you think the other person is thinking, to get it out of your mind as the observer and have them speak the words. This helps secure you in the observer position, and to see if those words are coming from the right person. Does it really sound like what they would say?

Remember that, as an observer, you would not use words like I and me, but rather, they and them, or him or her.

If you have a judgmental voice that insults you, see what it feels like to try to own that voice. As the observer, see what it feels like to place that voice in your throat and speak or hear those insults.

Many people find that it seems awkward. They prefer to send those thoughts off to some mean school teacher or bully that isn't even in the scene. That means those thoughts are gone and no longer even audible.

**Kinesthetic:**

Let's find out if we need to align the kinesthetic rep system. As you look at the situation, with the people at the right distance from you, hearing from that position, and thinking as an observer who has some distance from the emotions in the situation, notice what feelings you have.

Perhaps, even though you worked with the voices or judgments or thoughts, maybe some difficult feelings persist. If difficult feelings persist, shift your focus to feelings that you would really have as an observer. Interest, pity, concern, whatever you would feel, observing such a scene as an outsider.

Place such feelings where they seem to belong in your body. If you have strong feelings that belong to someone in the scene, place them back in that person and feel what it is like to really be the observer.

By cleaning up these voices and feelings, you are in a better place to be objective. It is easier to notice details and lessons from this situation that you might have otherwise missed. It can open your senses and your creative thinking.

Notice what feelings are the most resourceful. What feelings best support you as an observant, curious, creative person; a person who generates solutions and excellence.

This process can really liberate your subconscious mind as an empowering and problem-solving force. Allow yourself to relax in the observer mode for a few moments, creating some space for your subconscious mind to benefit from this objective point of view, and to feed in any of its wisdom as it becomes available to you...

The novelty of this can trigger subconscious resources, because the subconscious is always looking for ways to connect the dots, to help you pursue a meaningful agenda, even when you aren't sure what it is. And now, the observer perspective is a resource that you can draw upon whenever you like. It is not only a position for a fresh perspective, but also a safe position that can give respite from raw personal feelings.

## First Position, Self

Lastly, we will align the first position, the self position.

Bring your perspective back into yourself in the scenario. After all the work in third position, do you notice anything different about being back in your self position?

## Visual:

Check each rep system. Are you looking directly out of your own eyes? If there is any kind of offset, any misalignment, correct that, by shifting directly into your normal vision, seeing directly out of your eyes.

You should not be viewing the other person as you normally would. Adjust any submodalities you care to, such as brightness, clarity, and size.

## Auditory:

How is your voice? As you speak, make sure it is coming from your throat.

Of course, any internal dialog, thoughts and judgments should really belong to you and be coming from your mind, emanating from you. Make sure your thoughts are in first person, saying, "I think this," and, "I think that."

Your thoughts are not talking about you, they are coming **from** you and they are yours.

And your hearing should be coming directly into your imaginary ears. Adjust the placement as needed, so that it sounds natural and normal.

### Kinesthetic:

What has changed about your feelings? ...

Do you have your own feelings, coming from the normal areas of your body that such feelings come from?

### Final Steps

Do a final check and see if you feel aligned in the first position. Make any final adjustments as you like. You do not need to spend time trying to make it perfect. You are learning just the same.

Since we're finishing, and we know adjustments can spread, spend a few moments back in the third position as the observer, and see if there have been any other improvements.

That is the end of the perceptual position alignment process.

# What is a State?

I have good news. You have now experienced enough NLP that you will have an easier time understanding new NLP ideas.

You have already worked with what we call states. Do you remember when you created a positive state to get ready for a new challenge? You watched yourself in a movie and changed your posture, your facial expression, and other things that put you in the right state.

A **state** is the result of everything you are at a point in time. You've heard the expression "state of mind." What state of mind was the person in when he attacked the other person?

Was he so angry that he lost control?

Was it something he planned to do in cold blood?

Was he crazy?

Each of those mind states mean something different. If he was crazy, he needs help instead of punishment. If he did it in cold blood, then he's in big trouble.

So, while a state is your overall condition, a mind state is your mental condition; the emotions and thoughts you are experiencing; the clarity of your mind; the mental resources that you can access with the greatest ease.

# What is a Mind State?

Mind states are kind of like a smart cupboard. What if, when it was time for breakfast, you could open your cupboard and all the breakfast items were in the front. Then, for dinner, you open the cupboard and all the dinner items are up front. That is how states affect our minds. In one state, romantic ideas and strategies are most accessible.

In another, there is the potential to strike out and plot revenge. In yet another, there are all the strategies for office politics, making nice, and making sure your boss knows how productive and valuable you are.

Preparing the mind to be in the right state, or even the wrong state, is called priming in psychology.

# How can I tell what State I am in?

To create excellence, you have to produce the right state, so obviously you have to know what state you are in to begin with. You can size up your own state much like you would when you size up someone else. What does your body language show? Does your voice show stress? What kind of excitement or boredom does your voice give off? How tense or relaxed are you?

Of course, you can go into your mind and emotions

as well. What are your impulses? What is the overall tone and theme of your thoughts? What emotions are running through you?

Here is a little experiment for recognizing your current state. Take a few moments to think of all these things, and to scan your body with your mind for all the feelings that you are having right now...

Then, ask your mind to come up with a word or phrase that sums it all up. Let a few ideas come through, and then pick the one that you feel best captures the state that you are in right now...

# How can I get control of my State?

This is the art of state management that you are asking about; managing your own state of mind, or mind and body, really. Nearly everything you do to create excellence involves state management. It's one thing to have skills and ideas, but you take things to another level when you in the right total state.

This creates motivation, creativity, and charisma that do not come from thoughts alone.

# What kinds of states should I create?

Here is a great way to figure out what state you need. First of all, each challenge you face requires a different state. What I'd like you to do is to think of something you are going to do; something that is a challenge; something that requires excellence. It can be dealing with a difficult person, being in a sports competition, giving a presentation, anything that you want to excel at.

But wait; did you notice that I mentioned dealing with a difficult person? Most people don't think of this as an opportunity for excellence. But it is! Think of all the benefits of being in the right state for dealing with a difficult person.

In the right state, you will not be so upset or stressed out. In the right state, you may bring out a different side to this person that makes them easier to deal with.

In the right state, you may come up with creative ways of handling them or getting around them that come to you because you are not so distracted by the negative feelings that you have with this person.

So you should prepare for dealing with nuisances like that based on what the opportunities are, not as something that you just have to somehow survive and get through.

So pick your challenge.

What is coming up that you want to be in the right state for?

Now think of people who you feel would be excellent in that challenge situation. It can be people from history, people you know, even someone you make up on your own mind.

Now describe what state that person is in. What is their facial expression like? How is their body language? What kind of emotional state are they in? What else can you think of that is part of their state of mind and body.

Now keep running those words through your mind and notice that they can help inspire that state in you. Amplify that by paying attention to any and all feelings that match those words. As you learn to do this, you will find it easy to come up with all sorts of words that encourage a particular state.

Let's add a technique that you already know. Have a seat in the movie theater of your mind and watch a movie of yourself approaching that challenging situation.

Imagine yourself getting the posture, facial expression, stride, and other things that show that you feel these words; that you are building the power of those words in yourself, that you are generating in yourself the state of excellence. You have modeled that state by pulling words from an example of excellence. You are generating that state from your own words and from your own mental imagery.

Imagine what you can do after some practice, and by adding more of these powerful NLP techniques!

# What other ways can I elicit a state?

Many of the NLP skills you are learning build up your ability to generate states. Even becoming more observant of others' rep systems helps, because modeling can be so important in eliciting states. After all, it helps to know what states excellent people use.

Here is a method that you can use from your own experience. Over the course of our lifetimes, we have experienced many states. But we don't always feel like we are in the right state for a new challenge. The trick here, though, is that you don't have to have faced that challenge in the right state before. You can still use your experience. Just think of times in which you have felt some part of that state. Yes, even a small part of a state will help, because you can build a state from pieces of memories.

Let's say someone is going to give a talk, but they get very nervous and aren't very experienced in giving talks.

But they know NLP, so he starts by thinking of experts and what words describe their states when they give talks. He thinks of comedians, actors, diplomats, prime ministers and so on.

And he comes up with words like relaxed, confident, likable, smooth, proud, giving, sharing, dynamic, persuasive and on and on. He then thinks of lots of memories where he at least felt one of those qualities.

Each time he thinks of one of those memories, he builds the positive feeling of that memory in his emotions. The memories may have nothing at all to do with public speaking, but it doesn't matter, he is building a state of excellence from those memories.

Once he has built up a pretty good sense of that state, he imagines himself giving the speech in that state. He imagines it without sound, so he can focus on the state. If he loses the state, he can pull out of the fantasy and get those feelings back again.

As he imagines himself giving the talk, he imagines the members of the audience looking very positive and supportive. They are really enjoying the talk and getting excited about it. This builds his positive state even more.

Look at what he has done so far. He has modeled, drawn from memory, imagined himself, and even used the imaginary people in the fantasy to generate and amplify that state. Now he has experienced giving a public presentation in an ideal state for this. This is a completely new experience; one that will help prepare him to give an excellent talk.

While he's at it, he establishes an anchor that he can use when he gives talks. He imagines pulling the cord that sounds the horn, like when kids try to get a truck driver to sound his horn. You make a fist in the air and pull down. At the same time, he says, "Yes!" Now, when he prepares for a talk, he does that to get his state going. He even works it into the talk as a signature move.

Now you see how someone can pull together a variety

of techniques, like a chef improvising a meal, you can put various techniques together, choosing them to get the best result. The more techniques you know, the more you have to choose from. The more you try out, the more you have a sense of what works best for your various challenges.

# How can I apply these skills today?

**Good news! You have already learned important NLP skills.**

You can apply skills such as the swish pattern that you learned in submodalities. Now you're ready for more.

Now you have the key NLP skills. You have even gotten started with applications as you learned. We think that's really the best way to learn. In fact, many NLP trainers teach mostly through experience once their students have a basic understanding of NLP. Many trainings go from some theory, to stories, to experiences and demonstrations.

Although this is not a live training, our goal is to provide you with training that comes to you through these channels, and in ways that appeal to your primary rep systems, so that NLP will be very useable from this training alone. From here, it will be a matter of adding skills and gaining experience.

Let's start with what many feel is the most important

of all skills, one that you can begin practicing the very next time you have contact with another person. It's called rapport.

# What is Rapport?

Rapport is a positive connection between you and another person, or you and a group. You have seen lecturers, comedians and others build rapport with an entire audience. Perhaps you have experienced a good connection with a sales person, and by relaxing into that connection, found it easier to make a buying decision.

You've probably met people who had a strong, instant effect on you, either good or bad. What is it about the politicians and actors, the sales people, and the charismatic people you meet, that gives them the ability to create rapport? Is it just natural chemistry? Sometimes. But professionals such as politicians learn to build rapport.

Rapport is one of the first areas that NLP became fascinated with as it developed. The therapists that NLP studied early on had rapport-building abilities, but they had very different styles, at least they had very different approaches and personalities.

But, as you have learned, NLP is not content to just look at the surface. It models, it analyses and it finds the active ingredients that make things like rapport take place.

This is what you will learn next; the active ingredients of rapport; the ingredients used by professionals in many areas of life to sell, to lead, and even to heal others.

# This doesn't sound ethical. Is NLP just manipulation?

Although this is not a course in ethics or philosophy, we do want to share a couple ideas on this with you. NLP wants to see people develop meaningful values so that they can lead more fulfilling and meaningful lives. This does not happen at random. Except for the hero who is surprised by the heroic act that comes out of them in a crisis, most great people of history have done a great deal of sometimes painful soul searching. They have drawn from various sources of inspiration.

They talk about the feeling of standing on the shoulders of giants, even though history regards them as giants. Except for a few with very large egos, most of the great people in history confess to feeling like anything but giants.

But the things that they are proud of, are that they aspired to higher values, and that they worked to build the skills they needed to have a meaningful impact on the world.

We see the same thing in people today; people

who don't expect to be in history books, but who are fascinated by excellence; people who want to know how their role models do what they do. These people use rapport-building skills to achieve excellence in their chosen pursuits.

The first lesson in rapport, much like other NLP skills is flexibility. If you think showing interest in people helps build rapport, consider the person who is too shy to handle you showing interest.

If you think a dynamic, outgoing personality creates rapport, consider the person who would feel overwhelmed or pushed by that. If you think speaking from your heart and your vision generates rapport, consider the person to defends themselves with sarcasm and cynicism. What NLP has discovered about rapport transcends earlier efforts to build rapport with a list of personality traits. That is not flexible; that is a cook book approach. The master chef isn't glued to a cook book.

The second lesson in rapport is conscious application. It is not simply a gift or a coincidence; it is a skill. Since most people prefer to think that rapport is only a natural thing, they may be uncomfortable with purposely creating rapport.

We say that if you care about your mission in life, and if you care about your values, then you have a responsibility to learn to build rapport.

Rapport is part of your mission. You may be surprised to find that being pretty technical about it at first is very important. It's a little like a musician who practices scales for hours on end but emerges from this and other training with a great ability to play jazz. Rapport-building is the jazz of NLP.

# What skills should I start with?

Start your rapport-building skills with what we call sensory acuity. You have already started building this skill. We taught you to recognize what rep system people were using by listening to their predicates and watching their eyes and body language. Those are sensory acuity skills. Everything a person does is a message to you on how to build rapport with them. All you need is to know the code and the guidelines.

Have you ever been in the same room with someone and felt uncomfortable, or known that something was wrong, but didn't know why? With sensory acuity, you can describe everything about the person that was telegraphing signals to you.

For example, changes in posture can signal tension, extra skin moisture can signal anxiety or alarm, same thing with changes in heart rate that you can see from the carotid artery in the neck. The face creates brief flashes of facial expression that are not controlled by the conscious mind. This has been shown in research using high speed video. And those are just a few body language elements.

Consider speech. On the physical level, you can hear stress in the voice. A dry mouth is a sign of anxiety or alarm. But also consider the hidden messages in what people say. Their accent not only tells you where they are from, but their accent and vocabulary tell you their educational level. They drop hints on things like their feelings about personal responsibility and what kind of people they trust and don't trust.

**As you connect with people, pay attention to these signals, in fact, to all the different signals that people send off.**

A good cardiologist will tell you that when they started medical school, they only heard two things when they listened to a heart. Lub and dub. Lub dub, lub dub. But with experience, they came to hear all sorts of other things, like prolapsed valves, heart murmurs, and much more. So it is with sensory acuity. The more you pay attention, the more you will come to see, hear and feel. When you aren't building rapport, you can use this skill at parties reading people's palms as a diversion.

# How should I practice this?

A great way to start is with people that you already know something about. Notice how the various signals they put out go with the things you know about them. Then think of as many people as you can who share one of those traits, and what they had in common.

The next step is to rate in your mind the stress level of every one you see for a week. Notice how their stress level can change up and down in an instant. Watch for paleness, facial expression changes, tension, rigid body language, slight withdrawing in apprehension, how hard they are trying to act natural and so forth.

Here is something that will help you with this part. When people feel fear or excitement, they are activating a part of their nervous system called the sympathetic nervous system.

This does a lot of things, and you can observe many of them. Here are the most obvious ones: pupil dilation, that is, pupils getting larger; thinning of the lips, more muscle tension, paler skin, more skin moisture, more aggressive or withdrawn body language (yes, it can go either way), a tighter voice, the face stretched somewhat more, and faster foot motions, perhaps even being more on their toes.

These are all the things that the body does when it thinks it may have to fight or run away. Perhaps you've heard of the fight or flight reaction. Well, this is it; this is the action of the sympathetic nervous system.

When you do rapport building, you will see a very different set of signals from people. They are similar to what you will see in practicing hypnosis.

# Then how will I actually create Rapport?

The key to rapport is to adopt an overall state that is similar to the other person. You start by using your sensory acuity to size up the various subconscious signals that they are putting out, and telling you what state they are in. This is called calibration. Calibration is basically using the person's subconscious signals to know about their inner state.

Once you have done that, you can cultivate that state in yourself.

After all, people tend to like people that are similar to them. They can relate and they feel that they will be understood. They also feel some security because that makes you seem more predictable.

It may be a little easier, though, to simply start gently imitating certain key behaviors. This is called mirroring, or matching. This helps build your sensory acuity, because you have to pay attention to the aspect that you are imitating. It also teaches you a lot about calibration, because, as you imitate their key signals, that will tend to produce a state in you that is similar to theirs.

This is kind of subtle, but if you wanted to, you could go pretty far before anyone would think that you were imitating them. You will probably be surprised at how far you can go.

The only reason you do not go too far is usually that you don't want to have completely different personalities and then be in the same room with two very different people that you have done this with. You would be wondering who to act like, or maybe you'd suddenly need to leave because of a "family emergency" just to get out of there.

Let's go through each of the behavior-mirroring skills that are especially powerful ways to develop rapport.

# What about posture?

Posture is pretty easy. Without mirroring every single thing about other people's posture, practice adopting the basic stance or sitting position. Resting on the same arm (but as a mirror image, your right to their left) gives you a similar alignment. A more leaning forward, straight up, or leaning back posture match is good. This leaves out the more obvious things like crossing arms or legs. But you can try this as well, especially if it is not a person who would be looking for this kind of thing.

# What about movement?

Movement is another. What is their general style of movement? How fast, how much gesturing, how open or closed? Make your movement kind of similar to that.

# What about breathing?

Breathing is very interesting. If you match the person's breathing, it can have a powerful effect. It's a little harder than the other things, because it is an ongoing concern about timing; but as you get more comfortable with mirroring, start developing this match up as well. This is used in hypnosis and affects the timing of your verbal statements, as you're speaking during the exhale.

# What is Behavioral Mirroring?

In behavioral mirroring, you match behaviors that have symbolic meaning. They are mostly subconscious. In fact, the more subconscious they are, the better they are to mirror. After all, no one can think you're imitating them if you are imitating something they don't know they're doing, can they?

But what about being either masculine or feminine with the opposite sex? I mean, aren't you supposed to be different? Doesn't the opposite sex expect this? Well, yes and no. Remember, you are not completely giving up your actual personality. You are just adjusting certain things.

Did you know that when men talk to women, many tend to use a somewhat higher voice? Apparently many people already do a certain amount of mirroring, whether they know it or not. It makes sense that we would evolve with some subconscious rapport-building instincts. After all, these abilities have contributed to our ability to survive and to procreate. We know that the brain's neurons that are in charge of empathy and connecting with other feelings are called mirror neurons.

Autistic people have difficulty with rapport-building because they have less mirror neurons. Autistic people that are high-functioning enough to be concerned about rapport-building have to work extra hard at learning these skills because they are not as good with this kind of sensory acuity on an instinctual level. It has to start out as a much more conscious process.

Getting back to the idea of how we are supposed to be different across genders, consider this. Let's say a man is talking with a woman. She is a purchaser for a clothing company and the man is a sales rep for a textile mill.

He picks up from her behavior that she has worked her way up, she did not get her job because she was a college graduate with an impressive grade point average. He also sees from her skin tone and scent that, although she tries to hide it, she smokes. Her accent tells him that she is from a conservative and religious part of the country.

She happens to make a couple comments that are a little judgmental about people, comments that tell you she feels that people who are different are that way because they want to be eccentric or difficult, or just irresponsible. This is not someone you admit to that you are taking antidepressants.

The man matches her by displaying the qualities that she obviously respects, and mentioning items of personal history that match what she believes in. If he earned something through hard work, that gets mentioned in passing. If he has a degree, he completely drops the big words and abstract ideas from his speech, except for ideas that he can communicate in a very plain way.

She is from the south of the United States, and he knows that there is a literary tradition of commenting on things with dry humor, like Mark Twain did. He uses his humor in a plain but insightful and a little bit cynical way. His humor is at the expense of the rich, not the poor, and at the expense of marginal people, not regular people.

If he is church going, he drops a comment about his involvement. He may share things about going to visit family with his immediate family members so she knows he values family. Although he uses similar body movements, he does it with the kind of masculine quality that she expects, but in a gentle way that allows her to feel relaxed and connected.

While he's at it, he does the other physical mirroring that we have talked about, such as posture and breathing.

# What is Symbolic Mirroring?

Notice how we have gone beyond physical mirroring to include things of symbolic value. This is symbolic mirroring, and the symbolic behavior is often subconscious behavior. And we have seen that you can combine symbolic and physical mirroring. This combination of symbolic and physical mirroring is very powerful.

This same sales person probably has a wardrobe that is quite different for each area of the country that he visits. There is an engineer who happens to have autism and who works in the cattle industry. She wears western clothes, complete with the trimming and pearl buttons. This helps her have rapport with the cattle industry people that she works with. Since she is autistic, it is important for her to do what she can to improve her rapport. But it is an odd idea, an autistic person in a western getup.

Yet, this person became so good with rapport skills, that she was able to get the cattle industry to adopt a very stringent set of rules for humane treatment of animals. Her name is Temple Grandin. She used her leverage with the McDonalds Corporation, which does business with so many of the vendors, as a powerful strategy for inducing change.

This is a person who knows how to create well-formed outcomes. As an engineer with an analytical mind, she got a head start on how to do a well-formed outcome. Isn't it interesting how she has serious weaknesses as well as powerful strengths? She chose to go with her strengths to create a career and even engage in transformational leadership. Anyone who saw her as a child, unable to speak for years, and throwing tantrums because of her frustrations, would never have predicted her success. We know of an individual who wanted to become more persuasive to conservative people. So he wrote a piece that expressed some of his liberal ideas, but using the same language as the conservatives.

The result was that some liberals became angry with him for writing conservative rubbish. That symbolic aspect of the words he used was more powerful than the actual meaning of the words. Never underestimate the power of subconscious symbols and how they play with rep systems.

For practice in looking for subconscious symbols, look at advertisements. For example, when there is an ad for a drug on television, notice how the commercial changes when they talk about the possible side effects of the medication.

Notice how the music, acting, body language, colors and other aspects change to make that portion less memorable. Notice how they give the impression that the drug is highly effective, whether it actually is or not. In one commercial, the main character is a cartoon of a bee with large eyes. During the part about side effects, his eyes get very droopy.

# What are Exchanged Matches?

Not all your mirroring has to use the same parts of the body, just as your symbolic mirroring does not necessarily use exactly the same words. For example, NLP teaches that you can make a motion such as finger taps that match the rhythm of the breath, rather than breathing to the breath timing yourself.

This is called an **exchanged match**.

You are not exchanging body parts, but matching the rhythm or other mirroring aspect.

# When NOT to Mirror or Match?

There are things that you should not mirror. For example, if someone is getting aggressive and trying to be the alpha dog, you need to be more creative than just acting aggressive.

However, if you show an aggressive attitude about something that the other person is judgmental about, this can form a very powerful bond, plus, it can be fun to shout.

If you are comfortable with your aggressive side, you can adopt a posture that reflects that you are basically an aggressive person, yet not display aggression toward the person. Adopt a quality that is more like you are both on the same team.

This is a little bit like dealing with people who need attention very badly and don't have very good emotional control, such as people with borderline personality disorder. Mirroring people with very intense needs is much more of an art form and not a good place to start practicing.

If you need to, though, you can do mild mirroring of body language without giving the impression that you think your needs are greater than theirs. You can also, on the symbolic level, share the kinds of resentments and other things that the person tends to focus on.

By staying within the world that they mentally live in, you do not alienate them by intimidating them with a larger world. These individuals can easily collapse into feeling very threatened or inferior, and this can cause them to go out of their way to undermine you. This can include something called triangulation, where they pit other people against you. This can even include your boss, or legal authorities.

Rapport is very important with these individuals, as well as being well-protected against any ways they might try to undermine you.

After you have general rapport-building skills, you will be ready do use them with people who have needs that are more intense than average, if you are so inclined. This is especially the area of psychotherapists, physicians, and other professionals who tend to deal with people in distress. For example, you will learn that once you can gain rapport, you can use this to lead people or alter their state in positive ways. The pattern or mirroring and changing behavior of others is called pacing and leading.

With people who are suffering, you do not mirror their suffering, you just stick with mirroring the general physical and symbolic items that make them comfortable with you, so that they can feel okay about expressing themselves. If you feel some of the state they are in, that is enough to you to feel more empathy, and for them to know that you do.

Some of you readers, however, are already highly empathic, and can even be overwhelmed by others feelings. This can go two ways. You may find that mirroring is technical enough that it helps keep you from being overwhelmed or distracted by the other person's feelings when they are in distress. On the other hand, if this is not so- if you still feel too much of their feelings- then you are probably already mirroring them so much that you are inducing their state in yourself too strongly.

In that case, you will actually need to learn how to tone down your mirroring in at least some aspects, especially the physical aspects. Better yet, you can use NLP to find and change your strategy for feeling overwhelmed. You can start with what internal representations you have about the suffering of others. Nurses, therapists and social workers are often people who do a lot of subconscious mirroring without any training in it.

# But what if someone catches me mimicking them?

If someone feels that you are mimicking them, they are probably aware of NLP and mirroring. If they seem uncomfortable or offended, the best response is typically to back off of the physical mirroring, but maintain the symbolic mirroring without getting carried away.

# How does Anchoring work?

As you'll recall, anchoring is how we get into the right state for what we want to do. You connect a symbol with the desired state, or resource state. It's called a resource state, because you are more resourceful when you are in that state. Of course, we mean resourceful for certain things.

If you have intense confidence and desire for opportunity as a resource state, it would be very good for a job interview, and maybe not so good for being a grief counselor. You'd want to be in a somewhat different state for that. And you would benefit from yet another state to fully enjoy a Greek wedding.

Once you have your symbol, you fire the anchor in

order to trigger the associated resource state. This will be very clear once we have covered some examples. Perhaps the most commonly used anchor for personal use is a hand position, but you can get very creative will all aspects of anchoring.

**Anchoring** is related to something called behaviorism. Behaviorism tells us how to do behavior modification. This is the collection of methods used to train animals to do tricks; animals like dolphins in a water park that do back flips, and dogs in movies that put their paws up over their eyes. The amazing thing about behavior modification is that it does not require a conscious mind in order to work.

After all, it works on all sorts of animals. This means that it uses very powerful and primitive aspects of your nervous system in order to work.

Yes, it works very well on human beings as well, because we have the same brain components as animals do, though we have more. That's why were training them instead of the other way around.

When an anchor is fired each time you are in a certain state, your body associates that state with the anchor. At first, the anchor is a neutral stimulus. It doesn't do anything much. But once that anchor is associated with the state, you can trigger that state by firing the anchor. The trick, as you will see, is to get that anchor associated with the right state.

In behavior modification, this is called associative conditioning. Conditioning means that you create a response that happens every time there is a certain stimulus. Associative conditioning means that the response comes to be associated with another stimulus, in this case, an anchor that you can use to your own benefit.

Behavior modification is at the heart of problems like procrastination. That's why we combine communication with understanding the nervous system. With that, we can create solutions that run themselves. If you had to think about every strategy that you use for excellence, you'd run out of brain power very fast. That's why people don't usually get very amazing changes out of a self help book or TV show.

What people don't realize is that anchors are constantly influencing our behavior. Being in your workplace becomes an anchor for workplace behavior. Being downtown may trigger your desire to visit a favorite watering hole or ice cream parlor. Parents help their children get to bed and fall asleep by having certain things like music happen at certain times of the evening. It's called the evening ritual.

That's a good choice of words, since **rituals are anchors that help to trigger states.** The soldier who pulls out the locket from his girlfriend back home and looks at her picture is firing an anchor. It gives him some feelings of security and warmth. The non-technical word here is solace. It gives solace.

So an object can be an anchor. There is the action or ritual of manipulating it, there is the visual impression, the kinesthetic aspect of how it feels, and perhaps the sound.

# So anchors can be in any sense mode?

Yes, visual, auditory, and kinesthetic anchors are all used in NLP. Kinesthetic anchors involving a physical position or point to touch are very common, because you don't have to have anything with you in order to use it. Mental visual symbols or mental pictures are also convenient, as are inner verbal statements. Anchors can be external or internal.

External visual anchors can include a ring or bracelet. However, they may be diluted by the fact that you may look at them a lot without being in the desired state. So when it comes to visual symbols, we recommend using an internal one.

If you need to feel grounded, you might visualize a circle that appears to have been created by a Zen calligrapher. The nature of the symbol makes it easy to establish and recall, and it is not one that you would think of at random; it has a special purpose.

A person such as a great historical or religious figure might serve that purpose. You would put them in a special frame or something so that the image is specialized just for this purpose. You might come up with special objects or places that have sentimental or symbolic value.

When using sound as an anchor, again we recommend internal use. You can imagine any sound that you would not normally hear. If you go digital, a special phrase can do the trick. Prior to doing something that arouses anxiety, you might say, "Piece of Cake!" meaning, it's as easy as eating a piece of cake.

Kinesthetic anchors can be especially powerful. When you are going into a situation where you need to feel supported, you might imagine a hand on your shoulder, a hand that belongs to a historical or religious figure who is significant for compassionate leadership.

You can lace your fingers opposite to the way you would normally do it, so that it feels different.

You can make a pattern such as a circle with your fingers. You can touch a specific point that is not too awkward-looking to reach. You can even create combinations such as having a phrase and a hand position at the same time.

# Is ice cream an anchor?

This brings up the difference between a direct physical effect of a substance, and the associative conditioning involved in an anchor. You might be doing both with ice cream. Certain foods, including ice cream, trigger a reward center in the brain and create other physiological rewards directly. Chocolate contains a very pleasant stimulant, and the rise in blood sugar and the fat can be very satisfying.

When a stimulus, like ice cream or a loud noise, cause an innate response, the behaviorists call this an unconditioned response. But an anchor is a conditioned response, so if someone jumps when they hear a loud noise, the loud noise is not an anchor. Then again, there is a way ice cream can also be an anchor. Let's say your mother gave you ice cream when you had a sore throat, or you had ice cream with birthday parties and friends. Associations like this mean that ice cream, as an anchor, can trigger feelings of being nurtured, of being loved, or of celebrating.

The main difference is that an anchor works because it is associated with a certain state, not because it chemically causes that state or because it triggers a natural response that is typical without creating an anchor, like an animal hearing an loud noise and startling.

It's too bad more people don't know about creating anchors. Instead of using food or drugs to create feelings of nurturance or improved mood, there are many alternatives, and anchoring is one of them. The less resources people have to manage their states, the more risk there is of food addiction or drug abuse. In psychology, self-soothing is considered an ability that many people lack. Those people are at risk for addictions. Therapists attempt to help these people learn to self-soothe. Many therapists use anchoring to help these people. In addition to ice cream being high in fat and sugar, ice cream is hard to carry around with you. That alone makes it a poor anchor. NLP highly values independence.

# How long is an anchor effective?

Anchors can be effective for the rest of your life. The better formed they are, the longer they last. The better you maintain them, the longer they last. If you only use an anchor when you feel bad, it can lose its power to help you feel good. **A good way to maintain an anchor is to use it when you are in the state it is intended to trigger.**

You will learn how to do this during the next section where we teach you how to anchor. Behaviorism uses the word extinction for when a conditioned response fades out.

# All this theory is interesting, but how do I do the NLP Anchoring Procedure?

Here is how you create an anchor. Remember, the idea is to get a desired state a number of times, and to always have that anchor happening when you are in that state. Remember that an anchor needs to be something that is reserved for firing that state, so that it is not diluted with other states.

By the way, since one way of creating an anchor involves touching the client in order to establish the anchor, remember to explain this and get the client's permission first, so they aren't surprised. And, of course, you will want to use spots that aren't too intimate.

You remember what it was like to create a state in NLP, like when you created an excellent state for meetings and negotiation while watching yourself in a movie. Step one is to create a desired state. Decide what state you want to create an anchor for. Maybe you would like an anchor for that meeting and negotiation state. Maybe you have something else you'd like to anchor. Whatever it is, chose one...

Now recall all the times that you felt some aspect of that state. Watch yourself like you are in a movie, in third position. Every time you feel some aspect of the desired state, amplify it and expand it. Keep doing that until you feel as strong a state as you can... Each time you think of a time in which you felt some aspect of that state, see what is most visually positive and compelling...

Hear what is most audibly positive and compelling...

Hear any words that others said or that you could say that are most mentally positive and compelling...

Feel what is most palpably positive and compelling...

Feel whatever internal sensations are most positive and compelling, like feeling very up or expansive...

See yourself now, standing in a nice place, fully feeling

that state, and see how you look in that state; your facial expression, your posture, you can even add cosmic energy of just the right color streaming into your aura.

Now create a sign with your hand such as an okay sign, one that you would not do very often, or interlace your fingers in the opposite way from normal, and hold that position while you savor the state…

When you are ready, undo your anchor.

Remember to do this a number of times over the next couple of days to help strengthen that anchor. And note on your calendar to use that anchor for the next situation that you have coming up where you will need that state. You may be in for a very pleasant surprise, because anchors can make a big difference in your life.

# What Is most important to make this work for me?

It is important to remember the basic principles. Be sure that your anchor is unique so that it doesn't get diluted by other states and situations. Make sure that when you create an anchor, that the state is as intense as you can get it. An intense state creates the strongest anchor. The more pure the state is, without other things going, the better. The more precisely you focus that state, the better.

# How can I anchor someone else?

If you are coaching someone, you can train them in the same way you were trained to anchor yourself. You can also establish anchors just for the purpose of coaching. By touching a certain spot, such as their left knee, at the right moment, you can create an anchor, maybe just for a temporary purpose.

Remember that temporary anchor that Grinder created with the lady who was afraid of snakes? He basically just wanted her to quit interfering, and it worked. He associated snakes with the behavior he wanted her to stop doing. Here's a positive example of anchoring someone else.

Let's say you are coaching someone who is trying to become more assertive at work. They are so timid, that they can't even do role play with you, they can't even imagine doing it. In that case, you could have them imagine other situations in which they were, in some way, assertive; even just a little bit assertive.

Every time they do, you have them describe the part of their body that feels more free, expressive or confident, and you touch a spot on their left knee.

Now notice that I used three words: free, expressive and confident. You could say that for this client, you are combining three qualities into a state you call assertive. You are also emphasizing the kinesthetic modality, because this particular client accesses that rep system in order to get internal permission to be assertive. Let's say that you have touched that spot several times and so it is probably a useful anchor by now.

You could take a small, specific aspect of assertiveness, such as asking a coworker for their opinion. Just before asking your client to imagine that, touch the spot on their left knee. That is, fire the anchor.

If the client has an easier time imagining that action, then you have triggered a more assertive state.

Since you want to strengthen and maintain the anchor, direct the client's attention to any ways that they feel more assertive, that is, free, expressive, or confident.

Notice that, in addition to creating an anchor, we made it easier to practice assertiveness. Instead of role playing, it was imagination; instead of using a challenging situation, we used an easy one. We de-escalated the work for the client. You can gradually work into more challenging exercises from there.

Another way to de-escalate is to do something called fractionation. Just use one sense modality and blank out the others. For example, the client could just watch himself with the sound turned off. Then he could listen with the image turned off.

Also, if you add a positive ending to the imaginary exercise or role play, you help to de-condition the fear that makes assertiveness difficult.

# What else can help me anchor effectively?

Intention is an important aspect of anchoring. Intention can amplify the effect of anchoring. When rats were conditioned to associate a light with a loud, frightening noise, they learned to startle when the light went on. But when they became used to the loud noise and no longer startled, they stopped reacting to the light.

This means that the significance of the stimulus carries a lot of weight.

Your intention adds power to the anchor. When you trigger an anchor, be sure to use your intention to amplify the state. Don't just do the anchor and passively let it work on its own. Another reason for using your intention, is that this helps to prevent extinction, because you are guaranteeing that each time you fire the anchor, the connection with the right state is reinforced.

# What is the circle Of Excellence Pattern?

The Circle of Excellence pattern is an enjoyable way to free yourself of negative states. You will do this by extinguishing their anchors. We're talking about negative anchors now. After all, most of our behaviors have some anchors connected with them, including negative states. At the same time, you will be creating a powerful anchor for a state of excellence. This was created by Dr. Grinder.

First, think of an unresourceful state that you would like to be free from. Ask yourself what things trigger this unresourceful state. Those things are negative anchors; the kind of anchors you want to extinguish. To understand the anchor, look for all sense modalities, including visual, auditory, and tactile, that occur when you are triggered into the unresourceful state. Your anchor can be any or all of those sense modes at one time or in a sequence.

Next, draw an imaginary circle on the floor or mark a circle in chalk large enough to step into.

Now remember experiences where you felt powerful, creative, composed, or any resourceful state where you felt balanced and centered. Emphasize the experiences that you would say are good antidotes to the unresourceful state, that is, the states that would be best at counteracting that unresourceful state.

Next, you will slowly begin to step into that circle. However, only proceed so long as you are maintaining the resourceful state. If it diminishes, then stop and renew that state, then you can continue to step into the circle of excellence.

Do you remember how to amplify a state?

**Do what works best for you.** You can look through your own eyes as you remember an experience in which you felt that state. Remember the words; remember the feelings, posture, breathing, and so forth. If you do better seeing yourself from third position, then use that perspective and look at your posture, gestures, and expressions.

To make the state even stronger or to make it into the right blend, remember another experience. You can keep adding experiences and amplifying the state until it is strong.

When you are ready, you can step into the circle of excellence.

As you step in, remember the anchors that trigger the UN-resourceful state. Do this with each negative anchor. You can do this process with a partner or coach, who provides the negative triggers. Remember that you must maintain the resourceful state as you step into the circle.

What you are doing is making your resourceful, positive state more powerful than the triggers. As they say in behaviorism, you are extinguishing those anchors.

In the future, this circle of excellence can be an imaginary circle that you step into before a meeting or other challenge. You can make the circle so large that it is more like crossing a line into the entire area that you will be. After all, it is YOUR imagination. You can do anything you like with it.

# What is the Collapsing Anchors Pattern?

Many people say that the anchor collapse is kind of strange, but in a good way. The collapsing anchors pattern serves to free you from negative feelings that a situation or memory triggers in you.

The pattern starts by establishing an anchor for the negative feeling. Then you create a different anchor that is loaded with positive states. Once the positive anchor is more powerful than the negative one, you fire both anchors at one time.

The result, at first, feels strange. The person's eyes may dart around, as if their mind is trying to restore some kind of order or make sense of things. The end result is that the person is freed from the association between the trigger situation and the negative feelings.

The anchors are usually on opposite sides of the body, such as one spot on each knee. Placing the feelings in the palm of each hand, and then bringing the palms together also collapses the anchors.

Try this out for yourself. Once you experience it, you'll be able to have others do it as well.

First, identify a problem situation or memory that brings up negative feelings. Make sure you are pretty clear as to what troubles you about it. What do you see, hear, feel, taste, or smell that most bothers you?

Each time you sense that troubling feeling, press a spot on your left knee. Do this each time you think of another aspect that bothers you. Keep going with this until you feel that you have found all the aspects, including what was said and what you thought. Even include any really irrational feelings that can be put into words. Those are very powerful.

Once you have elicited that state and anchored it, you can move on to the next step where we anchor the positive state.

For this step, think of what states might be the best antidotes to the negative state; what are the most positive feelings that you could feel as a contrast to that negative feelings.

Also, think of what situations in your memories are the strongest contrasts to that negative situation. The best ones of all may be those in which you have what was missing in the negative situation.

It could have been missing helpful people or other resources, or missing good judgment that you have exercised effectively in other situations.

Each time you think of an antidote situation, press a spot on your right knee. Each time you think of an antidote situation, think of what makes it the most positive. Ask yourself what you see, hear, feel, taste, or smell that makes it positive.

Each time you find another sense or aspect, press that spot on your right knee.

Remember that you can find any number of situations to do this with. This is called stacking anchors. Keep going like this until you have developed a positive state that is stronger than the negative one was.

If the negative one was a ten, then get a positive one that is at least eleven.

Once you have this, and while the positive resource state is dominant, press and hold both the left and right anchors at the same time and see what happens…

After you have had at least a few seconds to experience this, slowly release the negative anchor, holding the positive anchor for a while longer.

# What is the Change Personal History Pattern?

This pattern resembles the collapsing anchors pattern. The Change Personal History Pattern works especially well for a person or situation that pushes your buttons, that is, that you have an unresourceful reaction to. In addition to the components of the Collapsing Anchors pattern, this one has future pacing and breaking state.

When you future pace, you see how a new behavior can play out into the future. This reinforces the changes, because you are seeing and feeling the benefits of a new state and new behavior.

Breaking state is a practice that appears in a good

number of NLP patterns. When you break your state, you refocus your attention away from your current state, and put your attention on something else, usually a neutral train of thought. There are numerous ways to break state. You can have the person imagine clearing their mental screen. You can have them do some slow, deep breaths.

Let's experience the Change Personal History Pattern first hand. First, identify a person or a situation causes you to feel and act in an unresourceful way. Be clear about what feelings and behavior that you feel are unresourceful.

Sum up the unresourceful state with a word or brief phrase, such as "irritated" or "shy".

Develop and anchor this state, as you have learned...

Now break the state by thinking about something neutral, such as how you selected your clothes this morning or the colors of the things in your environment.

Now develop a good resourceful state that is an excellent alternative to the unresourceful state. Anchor that resourceful state.

Now you will take the resource state (fire the positive anchor) into the negative state (fire the negative anchor)... and notice... how it has changed... now...

Continue to hold both anchors, allowing integration to take place. Release the first anchor (the problem state) and then the resource anchor.

Test the first anchor (the problem state). Notice any ways that it feels different now. If there is no difference, you can repeat the pattern, stacking additional resource anchors. Be sure to look for the most powerful ones. Remember to amplify the state using the methods you have learned, such as pulling feelings from each sense modality.

Now you can future pace. Think about what it will be like as your life benefits from this new behavior. Imagine various situations and opportunities coming up, and how they will be different. You can even place yourself six months into the future and imagine looking back at how your life has changed.

You can add a piece to this pattern when it concerns a person that pushes the client's buttons. Help the client understand the intent of the other party. This helps the client feel a sharper distinction between their reality and that of the other person. Many of the people who come to an NLP practitioner have difficulty with this particular skill; the skill of being very clear on where they leave off and other people begin. This leads to many of the problems that people use NLP for.

One of them is certainly the negative reaction they experience because they cannot tolerate other people thinking or saying negative things about them.

When working with a client, you can provide some instructions that help them do the pattern. Remember to say words like those I used when firing off the two anchors. "Take the resource state (as you fire the positive anchor) into the negative state (as you fire the negative anchor)... and notice... how it has changed... now..."

And when you test the anchors, notice any changes

in the client's physiology that can alert you to changes in their state.

# How do you chain anchors?

Chaining anchors is a helpful pattern for when you have trouble collapsing anchors. Sometimes, the positive state seems so far removed from the negative state that you can't seem to collapse the two. A good example of this can be found in the client who feels really stuck or de-motivated.

Trying to move such clients into motivation too quickly can really disappoint and alienate them.

The chaining anchors pattern can come to the rescue here. In this pattern, we will take smaller steps toward the ultimate goal of high motivation. In other words, instead of a two-step anchor collapse pattern, we will do a multi-step anchor chaining pattern.

You start the chain at each end, be identifying the negative and the positive states. In this case, we chose the stuck and motivated states.

You must exercise some care in moving away from the stuck state. As I mentioned, we need to move in small enough steps so that we don't lose the client.

For a small, but useful step, ask the client a simple question. Ask the client to tell you of a time when they felt different; when they didn't feel completely stuck.

The first useful step could be a negative state. For example, your client may think of feeling nervous as they did something that was different from being stuck. He might recall picking up the phone to contact someone in order to network. Although he was doing something positive, he mostly felt nervous.

Work with your client to define the other intermediate states that lead to the unstuck or motivated state. Make sure the client is coming up with steps that you feel are likely to be steps that the client can take: not too big, and not some kind of a detour. Typically, clients need three to six steps. Of course, people vary quite a bit.

Once you have these steps, anchor each step. You are just anchoring at this point. One way to have distinct spots for anchors is to use the knuckles; designating a knuckle for each state.

Test each anchor to make sure that it fires the associated state. Do whatever you need to strengthen any anchors.

After anchoring the steps, fire the present state anchor, that is, the stuck anchor. Then (not at the same time), fire the first step anchor.

Now break state. As you'll recall, this means to think of something neutral that distracts and changes the client's state.

What we hope to have at this point is our first link in the chain. Fire the first anchor again. If the link has formed, then the client will spontaneously move from the stuck state, to their first step state, but without you firing the second anchor.

Remember that you are not collapsing anchors by firing them at the same time. You are creating links.

Now break state again.

Fire anchor number one again. When the client moves spontaneously into state number two. When the client fully experiences this state, fire the anchor for the next intermediate anchor, state number three.

Break state.

Fire trigger number one, the present state trigger, once again. We hope to have two links in the chain, now. That means the client should spontaneously move through state two into the next intermediate state, state number three.

Break state.

From here, you repeat this pattern until you have linked the client into the positive state, the motivated state.

Now the client will have a different reaction when they experience whatever triggers their "stuckness". If it's the alarm clock, motivation will get them out of bed. If it's the vacuum cleaner, motivation will help them to enjoy a clean house. If it's that five hundred pound telephone, motivation will lift that receiver to their ear and help them network into new opportunities and success.

# What else can I do with anchors?

Anchors can go as far as your inventiveness can. NLP trained people have come up with countless patterns that use anchoring. Many of them are simply variations that practitioners, sales people, motivational speakers, ministers, supervisors, politicians and other people have come up with on the fly, to use as needed. Many of them have actually been published.

Speakers and others who must use state presence can actually use their position on stage or their gestures or other things as anchors to promote the needed state in the audience as a whole. Not only are anchors being used in such a case, but also emotions or states tend to be infectious in a group setting. If the speaker or presenter can just get that state going, it will kindle as part of the group process.

You can even use positions on a stage to chain anchors. Imagine moving an audience from skepticism or apathy, to motivation and wanting more. Add to this your ability to model the desired state by triggering it in yourself, and you can have a profound effect on an audience.

This method of positioning on stage has even been imported to the television environment. There is a famous political ad in which a frightening criminal was established on one part of the screen, with the politician on the other side. Then the politician he was competing against appeared in the same spot as the criminal. This is the famous ad used by George Bush Senior against Michael Dukakis in 1988.

In this case, they went beyond anchoring as NLP teaches it, and used human neurology in a cynical move to damage another person. This is a big reason why the public should understand NLP, they need to recognize when neurology is being used to manipulate people in negative ways.

# What is the Visual Squash Pattern?

Now let's take on an even more challenging problem. So far we have learned to deal with negative states, and even negative states that can not be collapsed with a positive state. Now let's take care of states that are in direct conflict. That's what the visual squash pattern repairs.

First, choose a problem that you feel conflicted about. This is not simply a negative state, but a conflict that keeps you from moving in a valuable direction, or a conflict that sabotages you or keeps you from making a decision.

Next, get familiar with that conflict. Delve into what the conflict is about. What is the dynamic? That is, what brings this conflict up, and what steps follow. One way of looking at this is to ask, "How do I know that there is a conflict?"

Think of the conflict as having two sides or two parts. Notice how each part sort of lives inside of you. You may notice that each part has certain feelings that go with it. Maybe a certain one of voice even, as you can experience when you talk from that part, speaking in favor of that part's agenda. Give each part a label.

For example, if you are having trouble sticking to a diet or exercise program, you may find a distinct part that is very motivated to do something other than that diet or exercise. You might get a label like Bacchus (the Greek god of partying) for the part that breaks the diet, or Video Lover for the part that would rather watch movies than work out. The part that wants to diet might be called Sex God or Adonis, while the exercise part could be called Buff or Powerful. Whatever works for you, whatever conveys the meaning of the part is what matters.

Now get a visual image of each part and place one in each of your hands.

Now we distill value out of the behavior. Get clear on how each part has certain values or motives. Ask each part what intentions and value it has for you as a whole person. The value of Bacchus would not be to make you fat.

That's an outcome.

More likely, it would be for you to feel satisfied, pleasured, and grounded. Maybe the eating habits also soothe your raw feelings, or distract you from stressful work. Boiled down, you would say that Bacchus is for something like pleasure, emotional stability, or stress management. Those give you positive reframes and open up your energies for transformation by unlocking you from the never-ending struggle against your impulses.

Ask each of the two parts what resources the other part has that would help this part. For example, if it was the Diet polarity, Bacchus and Sex God, then Sex God, the part that wants to be slender could tell you what Bacchus could do for Sex God. Maybe it's no fun being a Sex God if you don't know how to let your hair down once in a while and just enjoy yourself. You start with the part that you think of as more appropriate or positive.

Then you move to the other part. If it was Bacchus, he might say something like, "I would enjoy partying a lot more if I lost a few pounds, and, come to think of it, there are some people that would enjoy partying with me if I lost a few pounds."

This kind of commentary begins crossing resources between the polarized parts. They may begin to look, act, and feel differently just from this.

Now imagine what kind of part you would have if you were to combine the resources of these parts. What would that super part look like? Let that image form between the two parts and absorb more and more of the resources of the two original parts.

Now bring your hands together, completing this merging, and with your hands cupped, allow just the center image to remain.

Finally, use your hands to bring that image into yourself

to be absorbed into your energies and motivations as a force that will give you the power and choice that comes from these combined resources.

Now test the result. Notice how you feel when you think of the conflict situation? Notice anything that is different.

Remind yourself that this state is part of you and available when you need it. Now that you have experienced this new state, you may benefit from creating an anchor for it that you strengthen using the methods that you now know.

# How do I use Framing?

You'll recall that framing is the assumptions that shape how you perceive something and what you think your choices are. Everything we do exists in some kind of mental frame that contains a piece of reality. NLP is very concerned with not being too limited by the frame, and those who can think outside the box, as they say, can make very valuable contributions. The lightening rod, invented by Benjamin Franklin, was a huge step out of the box.

Instead of trying not to have impure thoughts so God would not burn down their houses with lightening strikes, people found out that they needed to use a lightening rod to channel the electricity safely into the ground. One of the best ways is to look at the assumptions we are making and ask what it would mean if each of those assumptions were wrong.

When people were trying to invent CD's, they had to figure out how to sell them. But nobody could come up with a good business model. They were stuck because they were in a limiting frame. The frame was that music discs should be the same size as what came before the CD. Do you remember what that was? If you're thinking cassette tapes, I mean even before that. I'm talking about records. They were twelve inches in diameter. But there was no good reason for the twelve inch frame. Everybody just sort of inherited it without question.

The big company, Phillips, knew that a twelve-inch CD would hold a vast amount of music: twelve hours worth. The licensing would cause it to be very expensive. And how would you know what collections of songs or concerts to put on it so that people would pay that much?

A fellow named Lou Ottens, who worked at a Philips audio lab, came up with the idea of using a much smaller disc. He showed his idea to the big company and the rest is history. The people at Phillips slapped their hands to their foreheads and agreed. Opportunities to create success by stepping outside of the frame happen all the time.

A person who can expand the frame is very valuable in business, leadership of any kind, and coaching. You've heard the expression, "Let's get some fresh eyes on this problem." That means, "Let's try and find somebody who hasn't gotten stuck in our frame, because we have gotten blind to our own assumptions."

One of the things people love about comics is that they step out of our frame and ask, "What if..." What if fish collected taxes?" "What if cigarettes were good for you?" "What if UFO aliens wanted to appear on talk shows?"

Brain science has even shown us that surprising humor activates a reward center in the brain, so, in some ways, our nervous systems are designed to explore and move out of the frame. But we are also designed and conditioned to think like everybody else. That's why we need NLP to get us thinking outside of the box; to liberate us so that we can create constructive surprises.

That's why the Meta-Model questions can break state and elicit an open-minded state. They function much in the same way that jokes do.

# What is the "As If" Frame?

The as-if frame may be the most frequently used frame in NLP. It is a good way to get around people's limiting beliefs. It accomplishes this by creating a way for the client to imagine not having the limiting beliefs.

Consider this example. A client says, "There's no way I can ask Sue to go out with me. Either I chicken out, or the circumstances just aren't right."

The coach responds, "If someone were able to do something like that, I wonder how they might get it done."

Did you notice how the coach created some distance by making it about someone else, and sounding very hypothetical about it?

Some people won't need you to do that. You can be direct with them, as in, "Imagine yourself actually doing that, and notice how you did it."

You can see some sleight of mouth here, in which the time frame or tense of the sentence changes from the present (where the coach says "imagine yourself actually doing that"), to the past, as if it's already done, (where the coach says, "notice how you did it.") That's a little like what one bunny said to the other. "It won't hurt, did it?"

A fun way to do the as-if frame that can really catch a person off-guard and produce a spontaneous breakthrough is to blurt out an as-if frame very early in the encounter.

For example, if the person says, "I'm here because I can't take it when my wife talks to me in a certain way, and I just go ballistic." Then the coach brightly blurts out, "Wouldn't it be great if you could be totally confident and relaxed when she does that?"

The client may experience a rapid state change, and may even start laughing. If not, the response provides more information about their limiting beliefs and their situation. Part of the sudden state change happens because, odds are, no one has ever spoken to him that way.

# How to apply Framing for Fear of Rejection or Criticism?

Like all NLP techniques, framing does not have to exist in a vacuum. You can combine framing with eliciting and anchoring resource states. Fear of rejection or public speaking is a commonplace opportunity for this. You can first elicit the state of fear by discussing the fear and having the client recall how they feel when faced with the challenge of potential criticism or of public speaking.

Now you can break the state, or you could say, massage the state, by asking the client how they know they are afraid. No matter what the client says, you can act surprised that they call it fear, because it looks more like excitement to you.

Or maybe the person needs to learn more about how to handle the situation, like what words to start off with. This adds some confusion and curiosity for breaking state and creates some transderivational searching for a more open mind.

You can begin eliciting positive states by getting their reaction to all the possible fear symptoms that they don't have. You could ask if they have defecated in the situation, or if sweat has poured from their body, or if they lost control and began running around screaming and colliding with the walls, furniture and little old ladies.

The humor helps to further break state and bring up some expansiveness and light-heartedness in the person.

You can elicit a more direct state of desire to do the thing by questioning whether they really want to do it. As they protest to say that they really DO want to do it, they are bringing the desire to the foreground.

Get them to defend that position a couple more times with more questions or uncertainty.

Let them convince you that they are really motivated to do it. The state of desire is a valuable internal resource state.

You can now present the person with a strong reframe. You have already mentioned excitement and needing skills as reframes for the so-called fear, and you have created some doubt in their mind.

Now you can offer the reframe that the intense feelings are the intense intention to get a fabulous outcome, such as getting up there for a talk and knocking their socks off, or being really charismatic and engaging with someone they'd like to ask out for coffee.

One of the things that causes this to work is that we are dealing with meta-level material rather than primary fear. There is nothing directly threatening their survival; nothing that they have to fight or run away from in order to stay alive.

So the fear is a daisy chain of internal representations that is triggering their nervous system. It's much easier to reprogram a flimsy internal strategy than it is to fight a grizzly bear. That's why I prefer to do NLP than work as a gladiator. Hey, there was a **reframe** for you, the budding NLP practitioner. Did you catch that?

# What Is the NLP Phobia Cure Pattern?

Fears, also known as phobias, can be irrational, but bother people for years without letting up. Psychology has various ways of working with these phobias, and medication sometimes resolves them. Trauma to the front of the brain even got rid of a fear of social activity in one documented case. But we don't recommend hitting anyone in the head; they could end up with a phobia of you.

Getting rid of phobias is important, because phobias prevent people from doing things they need to do. Also, people with anxiety can have slower reaction times when they are supposed to deal with a threatening situation.

At first, that sounds strange, because you would think anxious people would react to a threatening situation very fast, as a top priority. With too much anxiety, however, mental processing can end up being slower than normal. This means they may not handle fearful situations well. That can amplify their fear, creating a vicious circle.

The NLP has come to the rescue for many people with phobias. Researchers have learned that virtual reality can create the same fears as a real situation, but NLP practitioners have been using the imagination therapeutically from the beginning; and your imagination is free, it even comes with it's own software.

In this pattern, you will use the third perceptual position, and some basic steps from something new: time line therapy.

What we are going to do is to create a movie in the client's mind; a special kind of movie that eliminates the fearful, or phobic, reaction.

To begin, anchor a resource state, as you have learned. The best state will be one that is very different from having a phobia.

It helps to plant the idea, or reminder, that the client can learn in one single experience. We call that one-trial learning. You can also acknowledge the client's learning skills, talent, and abilities.

In a new twist on modeling, you now discover the strategies that the client uses for producing their phobia. You can use the logical levels of Dilts to guide you.

# What are Dilts' Logical Levels?

Dilts developed his logical levels to guide the process of intervention. Rather than focus on physiology and behavior, or emotional states, Dilts tells us to focus directly on strategies, sub-modalities, beliefs and identities. His levels help to put them in perspective.

Lets apply this to the phobia we were just talking about.

**The first level is about where, when and with whom the phobia occurs.** That is **the environmental level**. It is the context of the behavior. You can't really understand a behavior without context. After all, there are times that the phobia does NOT occur; there are people with whom the phobia does not occur. What is special about the times, places, and people connected with this phobia?

**The second level is the specific behaviors that occur.** This is the behavior level. This level helps you get specific in defining or identifying the behavior. It helps you escape the trap of vagueness that can help keep people in a neurotic tangle.

**The third level is capabilities and strategies.** How does the phobia get expressed as far the person's existing skills go? If they panic in an airplane, what skills do they use to channel that energy constructively? How to the prevent themselves from screaming and running up and down the aisle? Or are their energies expressed in utter chaos? The more capabilities that a person has that can serve as resources for coping with the phobia, the more complex and functional the person's behavior can become. Chaos looks more complex than organization, but that is because organizations use complex rules and abilities to stay organized. On the surface, they are usually orderly and appear easier to understand. In reality, they are complex and require exploration and study to understand their complexity.

**The fourth level is beliefs and values.** What can the client tell you about their conscious values that guide what they do around this phobia? The phobia itself may seem to the person to be very much counter to their values, but there is more going on that just the phobia.

There is how they react to it from this higher level. A good place to start is to simply ask the client why they do what they do. Don't just ask about the phobia itself, but what they do to cope, or how they avoid situations, or how they explain their behavior to themselves and others.

You can clarify their values further once you have this. You can ask them what they are trying to accomplish, or what they feel are their obligations or responsibilities in the situation.

From there, you will see that they have heartfelt values, and other values that seem to have been attached to them by their parents and others. Their values exist along with beliefs. They have beliefs about where their values come from and what would happen if they did not have their values and act on their values.

**The fifth level is identity and mission.**

- How does your client perceive himself?
- How does having the phobia affect his identity?
- How does his identity affect the phobia?

That one is especially interesting because the phobia

doesn't happen in a vacuum. The person's identity is kind of like an environment for the phobia.

The client might say, "Well, I'm a very private person, and I keep these things to myself. I will never fly on a plane because no one should see me like that. I'll tell my relatives that I'm helping a sick friend and can't come out for the holidays."

One way to get at the identity level is to ask who the person feels they are when they are dealing with the phobia, or what roles they are acting out; roles like parent, role model, employee, airplane passenger, and so forth.

**The sixth and final level is spirituality and purpose.**

This level addresses the client's connection to a higher reality. What is it that they believe about spirituality or the universe that guides them? This is an expanded version of the two levels that precede this level.

The previous two were of beliefs and values, and of identity and mission. This spirituality and purpose level exists because people tend to have this level of belief. Even non-religious people usually have values that they feel extend beyond them and define their place in the world.

Those values tend to shape their behavior as strongly as religious beliefs shape a believer's behavior. If nothing else, this level helps to summarize the way that beliefs and identity work together to create another level of meaning.

Does this all sound like too much to think about for a silly phobia? Well I'll wager that you already think about these levels more than you realize.

But these six levels help you to put such thoughts into perspective, and to ask some questions to round out your understanding; understanding that will help you provide a relevant response.

You don't have to spend an hour asking all the questions that go with each level. With experience, you'll get better and better at knowing what questions to ask which people. You will develop an efficient approach.

# So what do we do about the phobia?

Your next step is to get the client to travel backwards through their memories, back to the moments before the first experience with the phobia. There is always some time in a person's life before a problem started. Just realizing this can really help people. It may help them pin point how it got started. It may help them experience what it was like not to have the problem. Sometimes you get a pleasant surprise and the client has a major resource state come out of this kind of experience.

To help the client get more objective and not be too triggered, use the third perceptual position. Have him watch a movie of this time from the projection booth of the movie theater of their mind.

Now have them run the movie backwards to where they started it, and then forwards again; but when they go forward, run the movie in black and white.

At the end of this time clip, have them freeze frame and fade to black, like the ending of some movies.

Now the client is ready to move into the first perceptual position. Now have him experience the movie backwards in full color to the beginning of the clip.

Repeat these movie steps until the client no longer has the phobic reaction. That is, get them back into the projection booth, run the movie backwards and then switch to black and white, and run the movie forwards.

End in a freeze frame and fade to black.

If this method is not successful enough, consider doing the swish pattern as well. Once the client cannot bring the phobia up very well, that is, once the phobia is not strong when they think of what they are afraid of, bring the client back to the present, aware of their surroundings, and check the ecology. How does the client feel that they will be without this reaction, now that they can feel what it's like to be unafraid? What images of the future do they come up with?

This is future pacing. You may have more work to do with parts if the person does not feel fully aligned with this success. That will help prevent them from sabotaging their success, and it will help them come up with more effective and creative ways to live without this phobia.

Now think about what we have done as far as NLP theory goes. We have taken color out of the movie. This means we have taken away a submodality that the brain has used to encode the fearful experience. Taking away a key submodality disrupts the pattern. When the brain experiences a better reaction to something, it tends to encode that as being the way to go in the future, because the brain is designed to detect and act on the more efficient way, when it is able to access that effectively.

And I'm not talking about thinking, finding the right words, or being rational. I'm talking about the brain having a different experience; one that words and ideas can only lead it to, and they must be effective in getting there. That's why NLP has structured this experience this way.

As you gain experience with this, you can use this kind of pattern with other submodalities. Some people will do better with different submodality work. Sometimes a phobia will respond to a very simple pattern like the allergy pattern. For example one NLP practitioner named David Gould cured a phobia of baked beans by having the person first experience their fear in the presence of baked beans. Next he broke the state by distracting her with some conversation.

Then he had her imagine herself running away from blue baked beans. When she said that would be silly, he anchored that state. He had her change those bean colors again, and he anchored again. Then she had no fear of the actual beans.

# What about Modeling?

NLP models build on all that you are learning, and help you expand the power of NLP. NLP modeling let's you unlock the secrets of any masterful person.

Modeling is an essential part of NLP. It is one of the seeds that gave birth to everything that now makes NLP what it is. As I shared with you in the beginning of this book, the originators of NLP wanted to understand and teach excellence.

Fields such as linguistics, psychology, and cybernetics helped them analyze highly effective people. Much of the early progress in NLP was breakthrough ideas on HOW to analyze the behavior, seeing things that were not even seen be the very people that they were studying.

A key to how NLP creates models for excellence is to recall an interesting definition of NLP, that it is **"the study of the structure of subjectivity."**

This means that you look at how personal opinions and experiences are built. NLP brings together neurology, language, and programming as three key components of experience. Bandler had a great gift for modeling.

One of the key methods for modeling is to attempt to emulate the person you are modeling, but without any theories as to why they are successful. This causes you to perceive what you would have filtered out if you had gotten attached to a particular theory.

Since you have experience in creating states, you will

see that these masters create states within themselves to affect other people's states. Of course, you would expect them to generate states within themselves to harness their own creativity and skills, but masters understand, at least on an intuitive or subconscious level, that their state can help to influence the state and the behaviors of other people.

This is a huge part of the power of people with interpersonal mastery, such as master psychotherapists.

We haven't delved into language patterns very much yet, and we certainly will. Language patterns can have a tremendous impact on people. Masters apply language patterns to themselves, and they also apply them to others in many ways. You remember how important breaking state can be to an NLP pattern.

There are language patterns to do that and much more, without the client having to necessarily understand and cooperate.

This ability to move forward in a way that does not require conscious understanding and conscious cooperation is a great source of speed, efficiency, and power in NLP. If this sounds like manipulation, consider these two things:

If a doctor gives you an antibiotic for an infection, do you have to consciously understand how it works to kill the infection, exactly what order it will go through the blood vessels, and how you will metabolize the end products of all this?

Do you have to consciously know how to beat your

heart in order to maintain your circulation in order for the antibiotic to work?

Of course not, your body and the drug take care of this for you.

People who sincerely want to succeed will universally approve of a method that works, even if they don't understand it every step along the way. The subconscious is much too powerful a resource to neglect.

What makes this even more efficient and powerful is that you are training your subconscious to use these skills on you and those you work with.

The more you enjoy practicing these skills, the more you will gain momentum and abilities from your own deep well of creativity and intelligence. This makes room for your conscious mind to concentrate on learning new things, and to have a reserve of conscious processing power so you can create new solutions for new challenges.

Did you notice that we just talked about neurology, or states, and linguistics, or language patterns? As you know NLP stands for neurolinguistic programming. So the part that remains is programming.

**NLP studies how masters use neurology and language in order to create new, durable patterns in themselves and others.**

That is programming. It does not turn people into robots; it gives them new, successful choices that are available to them in a way that they can trigger. A well-programmed behavior does not require a lot of will power or thought to act on; it is more like expressing yourself or singing a song that you already know very well. But, since NLP understands the magic of states and language patterns, these skills are much more powerful than mere steps in a manual. If NLP had a slogan, it might be, "You CAN get there from here."

Speaking of powerful skills, one of the highly effective people that Bandler and Grinder studied was a famous therapist named Virginia Satir. When they told her what they felt were the active ingredients of her approach, she found it difficult to believe.

In fact, it was kind of disturbing to her, because it seemed to take the humanity out of what she was doing. She did not want to think of her self as applying technical skills that were effective on their own. But then, scientific exploration does not always flatter us.

For example, there is a good body of research showing that experience does not increase the effectiveness of psychotherapists nearly as much as one might think. Certainly not as much as highly experienced therapists would like to think.

In order to test this, Satir attempted to model therapy without using the ingredients that Bandler and Grinder had brought to her attention. Despite her heartfelt commitment and creativity as a therapist, this really hobbled her ability to conduct therapy. She was less able to gain rapport and involve clients in therapy. She was not getting the results she was used to. In the upcoming sections, we will tell you exactly what those active ingredients are, and we'll offer more from other models of excellence.

What is really interesting about this, as far as modeling is concerned, is that no matter what a trainer says about what makes them effective, you can use the universal principles of modeling from NLP to see even more.

NLP embraces not only what people think they are doing, but also what they don't know they are doing. In NLP, this is called a meta-model. Creating the meta-model of language in therapy back in 1975 is how NLP really got its start in creating public interest.

The playwright Oscar Wilde said, **"Success is a science; if you have the conditions, you get the result."**

# What are the key elements of modeling?

As you have seen, NLP looks through various filters of perception in order to analyze. For example, when we looked at a client with a phobia, we used the logical levels for filtering our perception.

By filtering, we focus our awareness in order to analyze. As we get better at this filtering, we also get better at connecting the dots and seeing the big picture. This is part of gaining mastery, as we discussed in the NLP model of learning.

Do you see how, piece by piece, we are building more

and more understanding and skill as we use what we learned earlier in this book?

We are drawing on this knowledge in various ways. When you use a piece of knowledge in different ways and in different situations, that makes the learning much more valuable. This is called generalization of learning, because you have an overall or general mastery of that knowledge.

When learning is generalized, it is not limited to just one situation; it is flexible and allows for endless creativity. As you can see, this book is modeling NLP as well as teaching it. Learning through experience, and modeling what is being taught are very important aspects of NLP philosophy.

To create a model of a person's excellent or successful behavior, the analyst starts by learning to elicit the strategy, or at least to understand how and when it is elicited. The analyst begins serving as a knowledge worker. That is, using observation and questioning to assemble the model.

Let's start with the observation of physiology. A master of anything from sports to psychotherapy displays a unique physiology, that is, physiology that is part of their excellence strategy.

They have a certain way of breathing and moving. They have a certain posture. It's easy to see how this would apply to a golfer or other athletes. But how could breathing play an important role in a psychotherapist's effectiveness? Breathing keeps them alive, you say? Of course, but I mean their pattern of breathing; how they influence their clients with their breathing pattern.

The answer to this question didn't make itself obvious. Even psychotherapists do not necessarily realize that they are using their body a certain way for a reason. Professionals who are very successful at establishing rapport with people use their own breathing as part of rapport-building. We will learn about this in the section on pacing that is coming up.

We also model by analyzing how the person creates their mental map of reality. What do they filter out? How do their values shape their behavior? Meta-programs and the NLP meta-model help with modeling as well. The simple way to put this is that we want to know what's going on in their heads.

In order to model excellence, we must know what strategies the excellent person is executing. Strategies, as you'll recall, are how people organize themselves internally and externally. In other words, how they sequence events in their rep systems, and how they sequence their behavior.

We can apply this kind of analysis to problem behaviors and painful states as well, in order to find the keys that allow escape from such states.

Consider these other helpful points.

When we model, we find out what really makes a difference. The rest may look important, but that doesn't mean that it is.

We also break the behavior down into parts that have

their own function. We also need to know which part is there because there is something about that successful person that only applies to certain people. In using computers to analyze the strides of runners, researchers found that the runners had unique aspects to their strides. The researchers felt that if they tried to perfect the stride of the runners, they might be taking away something that accommodated for some unique structuring of the individual runner's body. The perfection might actually slow down the runner.

In analyzing a terrible airline crash, the assessment team learned that the pilot had a unique and non-essential way of working the tail of the plane that caused it to snap off in a high wind condition, and that led to the fiery and fatal crash. This helped them understand that the tail was not defective.

We must also see what feedback the person seeks. Where does it come from? What adjustments does the person make, and based on what feedback?

A common way to do modeling is to imitate an excellent person. This helps us find out what is essential, because we can adopt or drop various behaviors, and we can pay attention to various kinds of feedback. We can also increase and decrease the intensity of various strategies.

# Once you have a model, what do you do with it?

As we have said, we use models of excellence in order to train others to achieve similar excellence. That can mean being a great chef, parent or anything else. We want to have a training design that is universal, in other words, anyone can learn from it. So the model does not exist as a finished product.

It must become a program for learning: a training. An important part of that training is the ability to train the trainers. The better they understand NLP and the NLP model of learning, the better they will perform.

# What is the NLP Meta-Model Of Language?

The NLP Meta-Model of language creates questions that clear up deletions, generalizations, and distortions in speech. Done wrong, these are called violations of well-formed syntax.

In grammar, syntax means the proper order of words in a sentence. In NLP, syntax means the proper laying out of concepts in speech.

The NLP Meta-Model is important for everyone to know, because these violations of well-formed syntax cause all sorts of problems, from everyday relationship problems to tremendous political problems. But by asking meta-model questions that clear up these violations, we also clear up our thinking.

They also help us see when another person's thinking is affected by these violations, so that we can be more in control of our own mental maps; our own sense of reality. With the meta-model, we are much less vulnerable to manipulation.

Here is part of a speech with a lot of deletion:

Back in the day, they started our country so everybody could be free. Now everybody's fighting and it could all go down the toilet.

That was a little vague. Who started our country? Free in what way? What is the fight he's talking about? What could all go down the toilet; what does that really mean? Now here's that piece as written by Abraham Lincoln:

"Four score and seven years ago our fathers brought forth, upon this continent, a new nation, conceived in Liberty, and dedicated to the proposition that all men are created equal. Now we are engaged in a great civil war, testing whether that nation, or any nation so conceived, and so dedicated, can long endure."

Now that was a lot more specific. But let's say that instead of a speech, it was a paper about constitutional law. When the word liberty came up, it would require a lot more explaining. What exactly is liberty, and for who, and what are the circumstances? Needless to say, around the world, countless court cases, government documents, and materials from civil rights activists expand on the meaning of liberty every year.

The meta-model helps us analyze speech by showing us the difference between two kinds of structure: deep structure and surface structure.

**Surface structure** is what you say, and **deep structure** is all that you know that is relevant.

For example, if I say, "I can't get a decent salad in this town," I might mean that the salads they serve are too high in calories.

I might mean that I have only been to three restaurants in my neighborhood in order to form this opinion. That would be part of my deep structure.

If you don't know my deep structure, you might use your own. Let's say my friend likes a salad with lots of croutons soaking in a lot of oily salad dressing, and plenty of chunks of cheese and bacon.

My friend would send me to a restaurant with that kind of salad. I'd be horrified by all the calories and wonder what my friend could have been thinking. Well, if we had both used the meta-model, we would have known what each other was thinking. The whole thing would have been cleared up in a matter of seconds.

The other thing about deep structure is that at its deepest, it is a collection of sensory representations that come together a lot like a chemical reaction. They bubble up and come together to form thoughts, opinions, and decisions. Then we put those thoughts, opinions and decisions into words. That's when we have the surface structure.

Those words cannot possibly contain all the impressions that led you to speak the words. This is why you must have habits, or strategies, for deleting, generalizing, and distorting them into something that you can say efficiently; something that will make sense and not take too long to say.

People who are very manipulative will hide the deep structure in bad deletions, generalizations, and distortions in order to be manipulative. If someone wants their government to be based on their religion, but they know that would not be popular, they can delete the bible and creationism, and distort it into something that sounds scientific, such as intelligent design.

This way, they can pursue a religious agenda that gets by some people. In the United States, high courts know how to ask meta-model-like questions in order to analyze legal arguments.

When they did this in the case of intelligent design, they stopped certain schools from forcing their science teachers to say that intelligent design was science. The science teachers were very relieved to know that someone was paying attention and asking the right questions.

If someone's girlfriend starts accusing them of looking at other women, and becomes very jealous, meta-model questions may reveal that the girlfriend didn't really have evidence, but her mind subconsciously collected some impressions that led to the jealousy.

The deep structure may have really been a need to escape some internal pain and to get more attention. Accusing someone of something definitely gets their attention. Unfortunately, in addition to badly formed syntax, the accusation also creates attention that is not very rewarding, and may even stress the relationship to the breaking point.

If the boyfriend uses the meta-model, the girlfriend may begin to see that she was really in need of something else. If the boyfriend knows NLP, he will give her attention that does not reinforce her jealous behavior, but instead helps to create a constructive relationship.

However, if the boyfriend does not have constructive strategies, and his deep structure references negative experiences, he may just get angry and act superior.

**Here, I'll give you meta-model questions for all the major types of syntactical violations, that is, poorly formed syntax.**

# What are Generalizations?

Generalizations happen when someone translates some experiences into a rule that applies to all similar experiences. Bigotry is an example we gave earlier.

Sometimes generalizations can go by without being noticed. If someone says, "Everybody at the party hated me!" you might ask, "Whom else did they hate?"

If she says, "Everyone had friends there, they just were mean to me," you know she is unaware of anyone else feeling uncomfortable there.

If you asked, "Oh, so they were sorry to see you arrive and glad to see you go," she might start thinking of exceptions and reveal one, even though she seems to be attached to the idea that everyone hated her.

This means that her poor syntax just opened up to a more accurate internal map, that is, she realized that there were exceptions to her generalization.

Now she has a resource: the knowledge that there are people that appreciate her.

# What are Universal Quantifiers?

Universal quantifiers are an all or nothing kind of generalization. If someone says, "Every time I do someone a favor, it ends up biting me in the rear," you might ask, "I wonder what it is about you that makes that happen every time, I mean, you know, since that doesn't happen every time to anybody else."

Your friend might come up with an insight like, "Well, your right, I need to quit trying to help people who are so out of control, because it spills into the lives of anybody who connects with them."

In this case, he found a universal source that gave the universal quantifier at least some truth. In this case, that could be better than finding the exceptions to his generalization.

# What are Lost Performatives?

Lost performatives make a rule without anybody having responsibility for it. If a girl gets a cut on her face, and a nurse says, "Now you'll never win a beauty pageant," then you have a kind of cloud of lost performatives. One is that she should care about winning beauty pageants.

Another is the implication, not a direct statement, but the implication that people will think she is ugly for the rest of her life. Another is in the nurse's tone of voice, which is telling the girl that it is her fault.

You had to be there to hear that part. If you consider the culture of the region where this happened, it is also connected with the idea that she won't find a man to love her.

Let's just take the main one, which is that she should care about winning beauty pageants. You might respond to that with, "You idiot, she's just an impressionable, vulnerable, wonderful, young girl with infinite potential, and she's too bright to waste her time running around with bimbos who try to be beauty queens. I'm going to get your fired for being such a twisted human being."

But that's pretty confrontive. How about this one: "Who is it who thinks she should care about winning beauty pageants?"

# What are Modal Operators?

Modal operators make a must out of a preference. Albert Ellis, the developer of rational emotive therapy focused on this one a great deal. People cause themselves a lot of suffering with modal operators, because, when the "must" is not achieved, they feel like some horrible injustice has taken place. It distracts them from finding creative solutions and enjoying life as it is.

If a client says, "I must have that woman, but she likes my friend," you might say, "It sounds like something really awful will happen if you don't get her. Tell me about that." He might say, "Well, that is the really awful thing. If I don't get her, that will be really awful."

You might say, "So if you didn't get her, you will be in a really bad way emotionally, really broken hearted." To which he might say, "Yes, I couldn't handle it."

Now you can go in for the exception, asking, "I wonder how many months it would take before you got your sense of humor back." His subconscious mind would have to have an incredible amount of restrictive control over him to keep him from clicking into exceptions.

You could add fuel to this. "I suppose you'd know that from how you've handled a broken heart in the past."

Witty quotes charm us because they toy with our internal syntactical violations. Consider this quote from Oscar Wilde, "There is only one thing in life worse than being talked about, and that is not being talked about."

# What are Deletions?

Deletions happen when the speaker leaves something out. When a person is being too vague or manipulative, deletion may be the culprit.

If someone says, "What a lousy day," you could ask, "What's lousy about it?" If he says he has lice, you now know he really DID mean it was a lousy day, since that's how the word "lousy" got its start. Unless you need to know where he got the lice, that's probably more information than you really needed to know.

Simple deletions are those where information is simply left out. You can't talk for long without making numerous simple deletions. After all, if you included all the details, it would take a long time and you'd get a reputation as a crashing bore; so deletions are a necessary part of everyday speech.

**Unspecified nouns and verbs are deletions that leave you wondering what thing or action the person is talking about.**

If a powerful local criminal says, "I'd hate to see what happens to your family, if you don't pay us to take care of your nice restaurant in our part of town," you'd say, "How much do I pay and to whom do I write the check? Oh, I mean, do you take unmarked bills?"

Maybe that wasn't such a good example. How about if someone tells your friend, "I was driving and here I am with this bad head wound." While he's taking his friend to the hospital, he might ask, "But what happened?"

Maybe it wasn't a car accident. Was he attacked? Was he being vague because he's hiding something, or is he being vague because the head injury affected his brain? If so, then we could say that the deep structure is the injury itself. Let's hope it isn't TOO deep.

But seriously, it is important to remember that deep structure includes everything from manipulation to psychological defenses to pure physiology.

Let's try one more, a nice plain one. Your employee says, "We'll be a little late delivering to the buyer this month."

You might ask, "How late, exactly?" With the information you need, you'll know whether it's an emergency, and how to handle the buyer. Otherwise you could really be blindsided. Employers and other leaders often get a watered-down version of bad news from their staffs.

That is a good time to trot out your meta-model questions.

# What is Lack of Referential Index?

Lack of referential index is a deletion where there's an unspecified party or an unknown "they". If someone tells you, "Everybody knows you're a liar," you could say, "Who on earth would say something like that about someone like me?"

That kind of backs the person into a corner, challenging them to disclose their sources.

Maybe someone does think that you're a liar or that you lied about something, but how could everyone think that? Has this person been telling stories behind your back?

At the very least, your meta-model question shows them that you can't be intimidated by such a cheap shot.

If you say, "Everyone knows everyone is a liar," then they are put in a position to say that you are some kind of special liar that makes everyone talk about you.

The more specific the person is, the more flimsy they will sound, until their statements collapse because the evidence is weak.

If the person says, "Well, the attorney general thinks so, and I have a warrant to search your office and home," the-e-e-n maybe you should go to the Cayman Islands where all your secret money is stashed, and decide where you want to live from now on.

# What are Comparative Deletions?

Comparative deletions happen when the speaker fails to say what they are comparing something to.

If a sales person tells you, "This motorcycle gets fifty percent better gas mileage!" you'll want to know, "Better than what, my skate board?"

# What are Distortions?

**Distortions are based on real sensory data, but they twist it in some way to create the wrong conclusion.**

If it's extreme enough, it's a delusion in psychological language.

If someone says, "A white car followed me all the way to the gas station, someone must be obsessed with me and stalking me," you might wonder if the driver of the white car was going to the same gas station.

Coincidences are distorted all the time. When someone hears about two occurrences of something, like a business closing in town, and turns it into a pattern, they might say, "Can you believe it, the whole down is going out of business. I'm moving to Brussels."

You could say, "I'm moving to Brussels because six

new businesses opened. That means we'll be overrun in no time! Two of them were opened by Pakistanis, lets go before there's no one left who speaks English."

Maybe that would be a little too sarcastic. You'd better know this person well before you get too carried away with what you are learning, or else you'll end up alone, and bitter, homeless and freezing. Whoops, I just made one of those distortions.

# What is Nominalization?

**Nominalization happens when we transform a verb or adjective into a noun.**

It also has to be something that isn't a real thing in the world. In other words, you couldn't put it into a wheel barrel. In fact, come to think of it, nominalization is, in itself, a nominalization. It's a noun that isn't an actual, real-world object. Some other examples include: accuracy, righteousness, superiority, excellence, and destiny.

You can see nominalization happen in old philosophy and old psychology texts quite a bit. That's odd, because philosophers have published material critical of this for centuries. Nominalization gets really bad when a number of nominalizations, or a chain of them, are discussed as though they were definite, real, understood things. When people do this, they come to all sorts of weird conclusions.

Here's an example. Someone said that atheists believe in a dog-eat-dog world. The deep structure that went on in their mind went something like this. Atheist equals evolution.

Evolution equals Darwinism. Darwinism equals social Darwinism. Social Darwinism equals survival of the fittest, which equals no compassion for those in need, a dog-eat-dog world. But social Darwinism is a political philosophy that only got Darwin's name attached to it because it resembled natural selection, which is a part of the theory evolution.

On each side of that weak link, the chain contains fairly good generalizations. Most atheists believe in evolution.

Social Darwinists believe in a dog-eat-dog world. But those two chains are only linked by a completely irrelevant nominalization. The verb "to evolve" becomes a noun, evolution.

Then, that noun gets attached to social Darwinism only because Darwin discovered evolution. The jump to social Darwinism is only possible because of word play. This is what we mean when we say that people live in a fantasy world because of acting like words are real things.

But there is often a hidden agenda behind nominalization. People who are not very introspective may not even realize that they are pursuing an agenda. The person who said atheists are dog-eat-doggers wanted so badly to feel superior to non-believers, that he came up with this as a response to research showing that atheist doctors were doing more for poor people than religious ones.

Outside of NLP, a word for nominalization is reification.

# What is Mind Reading?

**Mind reading is an irritating distortion. This happens when someone decides they know what you are thinking.**

For some reason, it's usually something pretty bad.

If you tell them they are projecting, they probably won't understand. If you tell them what you are really thinking, they may actually argue with you, as if they know what you're thinking and you don't. If they think you're lying, what more can you say?

So you see how irritating this distortion is.

If your boss tells you that you asked for the day off so you could sell company secrets to the competition, that's a pretty extreme example. You might want to look for another job, or get his boss to look at your boss' mental health. But most examples are subtler.

Let's say you have a friend that you have seen quite a lot, and you have done some nice favors for. It's someone you care about quite a bit, and really enjoy. But let's say you didn't come to their party, and now he's upset that you don't really care about him.

You know that he is wrong, and you know that when he feels better, he'll realize that he's wrong.

This means you don't have to take it personally. If he hasn't been drinking, you might say something like, "Exactly, if I cared about you, I wouldn't have let that bus crash into my car, or I would at least have left the hospital against doctors orders to get to your party. The IV bag would have been a good conversation piece."

But really, as a good friend, you want him to know that you had something that you couldn't reschedule, whether it was an accident, a final exam, or anything else.

# What are Cause and Effect Distortions?

**Cause and effect distortions can be sneaky. This happens when someone thinks they know what causes something, simply because the two things happened together.**

It's like the rooster thinking that crowing makes the sun come up. He must be right. It happens every time. People do that a lot with their emotions. They'll say someone made them angry, as if they have no responsibility for their emotions. Everyone understands what they mean, but people can go too far with this.

If they do it to manipulate people, as in emotional blackmail, then you might want to say something, like, "Even I am amazed at the power I have over your every emotion."

Or you could simply restate that you are doing what you do for perfectly good reasons and let them sort it out.

After all, if you don't give attention to emotional manipulation, and you DO pay attention to their mature, appropriate behavior, you will probably have a better time, and they will respect themselves more. It's good to bring the best out in others.

You could say that this is meta to the meta level, because when you produce a strategy that serves your personal well-being or higher values and then you have gone beyond coming up with cute responses to show other people that they are illogical. You have taken things to another level.

It is the understanding and using the meta-level that is important, not having a lot of snappy come backs that could alienate people. This section is to build your understanding, not make you think you need to be sarcastic or directly confrontative all the time in real life.

# What are Presuppositions?

**Presuppositions are the hidden ideas in a statement.**

If someone asks you if you have stopped beating your spouse, they are presupposing that you beat your spouse. And that's assuming that you have one to beat.

You could say, "You should know, or haven't you spoken with your mother lately?" but we wouldn't advise that.

Maybe you could say, "I never started, but I hear

it's hard to stop once you start, have you considered a support group?"

# What is Complex Equivalence?

**Complex equivalence connects two ideas that don't belong together.**

For example, if your client is too upset about an argument with her son, she might say, "I can't believe I told him he was lazy, now he'll be traumatized forever."

You could respond with questions about the kind of stresses that he has survived, and how he was recovered from them, maybe even how they have helped to build his character.

You could discuss ways to get over the argument and build better agreements about his responsibilities and the consequences of good and bad behavior.

You could talk about how to create more consistent rules at home and how this benefits everyone. One of the best says to help with complex equivalence, is to supportively approach the issue from several factual and positive directions, as in the example above.

# How can I use the Meta-Model for therapy?

The creators of motivational interviewing have created two very helpful elements that can be used in Meta-Model responses that are quite therapeutic, and that protect the therapeutic relationship between a therapist and client. Coaches can use this as well.

This approach causes the client to make progressive, mature statements instead of the therapist. This eliminates resistance, and creates healing momentum within the client.

The first technique is what we call **negative spotlighting.** When a person says something that violates well-formed syntax, you can exaggerate this to highlight it so that the other person will model their world more effectively.

For example, if a drug addict says, "I don't need to be a purist. I can have some cocaine once in a while."

You can say, "So you are now totally in control of cocaine." If the person has been in a recovery program, they know this is ridiculous. They have to say something like, "Well, uh, I guess that's just the addiction talking."

Notice that the other person said it, not you. You only used the motivational interviewing technique to mirror back what they said in a way that they could not support.

Although the practitioner's statement is kind of an

exaggeration, it is not done with the least bit of sarcasm. It has to be done in a completely straight-faced and gentle manner. It is said in a factual tone. Not, "Oh, so you think you can control cocaine now, huh?"

It's a flat statement of fact.

"So, you are now totally in control of cocaine." You say it smoothly and plainly, maybe even a little like it's new information. This way, the client can correct you and enlighten you.

That tells the client that he is insightful and has something to contribute. It gives the client the experience of coming to his own conclusions, and a sense of controlling his own thoughts to change his direction in a positive way. This creates more flexibility in the client's thinking.

This is very helpful because now the client owns the more enlightened statement; they do not feel compelled to resist you, because you are not trying to shove it down their throat.

Any time you feel like you are pushing a client or customer, you could probably benefit from a motivational interviewing technique. The original book on this is called Motivational Interviewing.

The other motivational interviewing technique that is a great Meta-Model response, we call positive spotlighting. Here, you highlight something very constructive or adaptive that the client says.

This reinforces the constructive way of thinking, and gives them credit. If the person says, "I realized that my wife left me because I was abusing drugs," you could say, "You have the kind of insight that shows real courage in the face of a tremendous loss."

Isn't that much better than saying, "So you're finally realizing what a schmuck you've been!"?

This positive approach reinforces the best qualities of the person and creates hope and strength that could make the difference between sobriety and relapse, perhaps even life and death.

This is not to say that you bear total responsibility for every choice a client, customer, or employee makes, but I say it to remind you of what an important contribution you can make to people's lives when you learn the powerful insights and methods of NLP.

# What is The Milton Model?

Early in the development of NLP, the developers modeled a famous hypnotherapist and physician named **Milton H. Erickson.** He is quite legendary in the field of psychotherapy, especially in clinical hypnosis.

# Why use Hypnosis in NLP?

First please understand that hypnosis offers much more than the stereotypes you may have run across. Hypnosis doesn't just happen on a stage where you make someone act like a chicken, and it is not just making someone slee-e-py and programming them to stop smoking.

Because **NLP is about modeling**, NLP has drawn several important things from hypnosis. The language and methods that Erickson used has value on various forms of persuasion and stress management, as well as treating mental health issues. Much of it has nothing to do with going into deep trances.

# Who was Milton Erickson?

Milton H. Erickson, MD lived from 1901 to 1980. He was a psychiatrist who provided medical hypnosis and family therapy. People love to tell the many stories about his unconventional and innovative methods as a psychotherapist. The book **Uncommon Therapy**, by Jay Haley has many fascinating stories about his work, and was a best-selling book. He pioneered brief therapy methods, and even coined the term "brief therapy".

He achieved his results by blending together numerous things he knew about, like systems theory, behavior modification, and the subconscious mind. He saw the subconscious mind as being a creative, solution-generating force all on its own.

Much of his work was about bringing subconscious resources into play for therapeutic purposes. People often had no idea what he did or how he did it, but experienced tremendous improvements in their lives and symptoms. He had a big impact on psychotherapy beginning in the 1950's.

When he was seventeen, Erickson contracted polio, and nearly died. Recovery was very difficult. Regaining his ability to move, and dealing with chronic pain led him to use various psychological and trance techniques. Because his resulting intense interest in psychology, he got a degree in psychology while he was in medical school.

Erickson also credited his dyslexia, tone deafness, and color blindness with causing him to pay attention to communication patterns that other people overlooked.

Because of Erickson's reputation in hypnosis, Gregory Bateson and Margaret Mead had him analyze films of trance states in Bali. Later Bateson consulted with him on communication patterns. It was through Bateson that Erickson met Bandler, Grinder, and Jay Haley.

After this, Bandler and Grinder began modeling Erickson.

# What is Hypnosis?

It is difficult to define hypnosis, because it can take various forms, and even experts have varying definitions. A good working definition is that hypnosis is a state of inner absorption that can include intense focus or free reverie. Hypnosis is distinguished from a trance state in that it is guided by the hypnotist, usually for therapeutic purposes. Stage hypnosis may involve actual hypnosis, or participants acting out impulses while on the spot to be entertaining.

An amusing dialog that would go one between Bandler and Grinder on the question of the definition of hypnosis, was a debate over whether everything was hypnosis or nothing was really hypnosis. This was not only a way of making important points about hypnosis, but also inducing hypnosis in the audience as a teaching technique.

A key point was that trance is really a matter of degree, and all communication influences your mind by creating artificial experiences of some kind.

There are two sources of confusion here. One is that influencing the subconscious mind is not necessarily hypnosis. That's because subliminal influence and hypnosis are not the same thing. The other is that NLP has drawn things from hypnosis that do not involve trance or hypnotic phenomena, or may only involve brief periods of light trance.

# What is a Trance?

In trance, the person is not conscious in the typical sense. At most, the person is conscious of being observant, and fairly free of thoughts and judgements, or of a stream of thoughts or reverie, carrying him away from the present moment. This state allows a hypnotist to have more influence on the subconscious mind, because the conscious mind is not able to get in the way and subvert solutions that are not acceptable for some reason.

This may sound like it would cause a problem with the person's ecology, but when a serious problem resolves through the subconscious, the person's conscious mind tends to go along. This is because the conscious mind, though normally acting as a gate keeper, is only taking that role as the result of subconscious adaptations. Once the subconscious is aligned and using the right resources, the conscious mind no longer acts out the subconscious problems.

This does not mean that hypnosis can easily change a well-thought-out or deeply ingrained opinion or tradition. Hypnosis is for things that do not have a strong conscious structure, but rather, it is for dysfunctional patterns with subconscious roots. The conscious mind may appear to be the cause, but that is only because the conscious creates pretexts for subconscious motivations in order to preserve for a person a coherent sense of identity. In other words, the conscious mind takes credit, but it is not really the cause.

Trance is not an either-or phenomenon; we are in various degrees of trance all the time. We range from being very clear-headed and responsive to our environment in general, to drifting into a mild reverie, to drifting into a daydream, to drifting off altogether.

You do not have to go through a formal induction process in order to experience hypnosis. Erickson was famous for creating and utilizing trance through conversational hypnosis.

# If Rapid, Brief Trance is Really Possible, Show Me One.

You can have a brief trance experience that you ARE aware of right now, and you can come out of it right away as well.

If you are driving or doing anything dangerous such as cutting vegetables, skip past this for later (you shouldn't be doing these things while reading anyway!). Otherwise, control this experience by sitting or lying down, and participating in a manner that you find comfortable, such as by becoming aware of how your shoulders gently expand as you exhale, and feel their natural weight as you exhale.

This allows you to experience the relaxation that occurs as you exhale, such as how the surface you are on presses up to suspend you in space. This makes it easier to sense how other muscles can allow your full weight onto the surface, including the gentle expansion of the back of your neck.

I know that you sometimes think about the healthy things that you do, even the ones that you do more or less consistently, and so it isn't much more to think of how you would like to look twenty years from now. Your imagination allows you to create an ideal image in some way.

You can see yourself in very desirable activities, and enjoying the attention of other witty, active people. Your subconscious mind can continue creating these excellent conditions as you go through your life, enjoying other activities like studying NLP. Yes, you can take this creativity with you as a background program that creates your excellent life. To begin, notice your environment, its sounds and feelings. And as you look through your eyes, notice the colors around you.

As this creates more alertness in you, you can take a breath and stretch, fully restoring your alertness and connection with your environment.

# What is Conversational Hypnosis?

Erickson championed the idea NLP calls conversational or covert hypnosis. Instead of setting up a formal induction and requiring the patient to concentrate in some fashion, Erickson would produce trance in his patients through normal-seeming interaction.

In the hypnosis field, this is called naturalistic hypnosis. Bandler and Grinder modeled this mysterious and provocative approach.

Since the patient may not be aware that it is taking place, and may not even remember it, it can be called covert hypnosis. They were fascinated with the idea that the power of the subconscious mind could be utilized in what appeared to be such an off-hand method.

# What about the role of the Subconscious in hypnosis?

As you'll recall the subconscious mind is everything in your mind that you are not aware of. As we described while introducing Milton Erickson, the subconscious mind can also be a source of creative solutions. You might think of the subconscious as being a really big room, and your conscious mind as being a flashlight.

On second thought, make that a room with some external rooms, since your conscious mind can't directly perceive everything in your subconscious, since some of that is called the subconscious.

The subconscious is so **sub-conscious** that it is nearly impossible to become aware of. Highly intuitive and artistic people work with their subconscious somewhat like someone navigating in a boat. They don't control it, exactly. Certainly not the way you would control a car. But they manage conditions that influence it, and they get to their destination. On the other hand, they also learn to interpret the signals from their subconscious minds, even though the communication is not as clear and direct as it is through conscious communication.

Over time, intuitive and artistic people have learned to trust their subconscious minds, and this means gaining intimacy with the signals that the subconscious mind offers to the conscious mind.

NLP understands that the subconscious is a source of creative solutions. This is key to the Milton model.

# What is the Milton Model good for?

As we mentioned, there are various benefits from hypnosis as practiced by Milton Erickson, and there are still more benefits that NLP derived from Erickson's work that are not necessarily hypnosis; at least they do not involve prolonged trance states.

Because of its diverse elements and flexibility, the Milton model can be used in some fashion in nearly all communication challenges. These include persuasion, sales, psychotherapy, rapport-building, breaking a state, creating brief and useful trance states, stress management and self-hypnosis.

We will look at a whole tool box full of Milton model techniques, including something called transderivational search. As you'll recall, rapport-building is very important in NLP, because it supports all communication. Erickson's abilities in this area, largely based on rapid trance induction are key parts of NLP.

# What is Transderivational Search?

**Transderivational search**, which we will call TDS, is a little like a search you can do on a computer, except that it is looking for even vague matches. To do this, something called fuzzy logic is used. The human mind is great at fuzzy logic.

In fact, it is so good at it that it may come up with vague matches and give them more power than it should. This gives even fairly inept Tarot card readers a great deal of credibility as the mind of the person whose cards are being read makes sense out of what the reader is saying. The mind comes up with various memories and situations that match the general statements of the reader. This can be a very convincing experience.

Nonetheless, we really do need our TDS abilities. We make decisions by assembling related sensory information, and we need TDS in order to assemble them and derive a decision. It is TDS that gives us the ability to work quickly with incredibly large amounts of life experience, and it is TDS that gives us flexibility in our responses that no present day machine can approach.

One of the useful things about TDS from an NLP point of view is that it generates a brief trance state while it occurs. Stage psychics actually generate repeated brief trance states in their subject, and then kindle the trance into a focused, involved, and credulous, that is, easy belief, state. You can see this in some sales presentations as well. Psychotherapists may use this to help clients become more open minded, but the therapist may have no idea they are doing this.

# How can I actually use the Milton Model?

We will teach you the Milton model by showing you a number of techniques from the model. We'll also provide examples of how to use the techniques.

# What are Meta-Model Violations?

Erickson's work goes completely against the direction of the NLP meta-model. While the meta-model gets at more specific knowledge, Erickson's work takes people to higher levels of abstraction, to values that are more general. He used a great deal of vague language that was extraordinarily good at shaping the states and directing the resources of his patients.

You can find all of the meta-model violations sprinkled throughout the text of Erickson's hypnotic work. As you learn the patterns of the Milton model that follow, you will see that they contain strategic meta-model violations.

# What is Pacing Current Experience?

We have talked quite a bit about rapport building, and pacing was a key part of that. Pacing the breath, that is, breathing at the same rate as someone else, is an example. What you say is also a really important resource for pacing. When you pace a person's current experience, you are simply bringing their experience into what you are saying somehow. This makes what you are saying more invisible and trustworthy at the same time. It creates a kind of momentum that gives power to other things you will say.

For example, "As you feel the surface you are on, and hear the sound of my voice, the relaxation you're starting to feel allows you to take an easy, slow breath."

# What are Pacing and Leading?

Once you have done enough pacing, the person is ready for you to not merely MATCH their state with pacing, but to LEAD them into whatever state is necessary for what you are doing. As in the previous example, where we insert an easy, slow breath, we are encouraging deeper relaxation.

Notice that we don't tell the person to relax; we cultivate a state of relaxation by supporting the physiology of relaxation. Better yet, we are pacing and leading at the same time, because we timed the easy slow breath with one that was already taking place in the other person.

That means that that was just the beginning of leading, where we are punching up the awareness of the state that we want to increase. This is called kindling, where an existing state is reinforced and supported so that it will become dominant and rise above the other states that are, in a sense, competing for dominance in the person.

As the state increases, your leading can become

increased as well, as with the statement, "As your relaxation deepens, the remaining muscles that feel some tension can absorb this relaxation, making your inhale seem to fill more of your body."

# What are Linking Words?

Erickson used words called conjunctions, words such as "and" in pacing and leading. He linked the pacing with the leading in a way that made it all seem to belong together, and this gave his leading commands a lot of impact.

Consider this example. "As you experience this training, and wonder how >>you will apply it successfully, you hear the sound of my voice providing the information so that >>you can enjoy mastery."

The pacing was that you experience this training, and that you wonder how successful you'll be.

This last bit about wondering can inspire a transderivational search for anything you are wondering about and any ways that this training may make you feel challenged. Brining up any doubts that you have about yourself and then embedding the command that "you will apply it successfully" is a mild anchor collapse as well as trance reinforcer. Nonetheless, the statement that "you are wondering" is also pacing your actual experience.

Then I said, "you hear the sound of my voice providing the information" which is still pacing. I finished with "so that you can enjoy mastery." Giving the purpose of the information doesn't seem like leading, but as you probably noticed, it is really a command to enjoy mastery. That is leading disguised as a simple statement about information.

As you can tell, we are not only training you on a simple technique, but showing you how you can blend several techniques together.

With experience, NLP practitioners' skills become so multilayered that they rely on their subconscious minds to do most of the work. When they listen to transcripts of their own work, they can be surprised to hear how many techniques they are actually using at the same time. I say this because you can trust that this will happen for you as well.

Remember that Milton Erickson had some very serious impairments, including pain and dyslexia, as well as delayed development because of polio. Yes, he was very bright, but there are plenty of people who have learned these techniques who aren't particularly bright. Not that I would say who they are.

# What is Disjunction?

Disjunction is a lot like linking, but it makes a contrast or choice while it slips in an embedded command or leading statement.

For example, "I don't know whether you will give your

full attention to this section, or think of some other useful information from your experiences, or even relax and learn while in a deeply relaxed state." In this example all three options are desirable.

But it starts out as if I would say, "I don't know whether you will give your full attention or not." Of course, the implied "not" can bring up any feelings of resistance or self doubt about one's ability to focus and pay attention.

Now we have some transderivational search contributing to the trance and open-mindedness. But we also have the unexpected shift into a very different statement.

This kind of unexpected shift can also contribute to trance, instead of simply causing alertness, because the wording continues to simply take the form of choices that more or less pace the person's experience. The actual choices that follow, of drawing from experience or learning while in trance aren't actually much of a contrast with the first option of paying attention, are they?

Instead, they do utilization: utilization of the mind wandering.

Why not remind the subconscious, if it is going to wander, to bring up useful experiences, or to learn while the conscious mind is distracted?

You can try this with volunteers among your friends, telling them that you'd like them to tell you if they notice you giving them three choices that aren't exactly choices. It can be a game and they can learn with you.

# What are Implied Causes?

This technique is a little like the previous ones, by pacing and leading using a simple connection. Implied Causes is a technique that uses words that imply that one thing will lead to another.

I might say, "As you take in all this information, you can know that your mind will digest it into useful wisdom in time. Knowing you have a subconscious mind gives you time to relax and enjoy learning."

That doesn't really exactly make sense, does it? You have whatever time you have, knowing you have a subconscious mind doesn't actually give you time. But I created an implied cause there, and it was intended to help the student of NLP learn more effectively by being more relaxed about it.

Since people can feel anxiety as they learn, that can make them really enjoy the contrast of relaxing into learning that will occur over a period of time. Now there's an implied cause. That anxiety will make you relax. Let me say part of that again; see how that worked as an implied cause.

"Since people can feel anxiety as they learn, that can make them really enjoy the contrast of relaxing into learning."

The words that usually occur in implied causes are

since, when, while, as, after, often, before, during, following, and throughout.

Before you learn through relaxation, you might want to sit in an even more comfortable position.

When you become aware of the sounds around you, you can realize that your relaxation is a powerful force for focus and learning.

While you are hearing these examples of implied causes, your subconscious mind has been busy creating understanding that your conscious mind do whatever it wants to as you learn even more.

# What are Tag Questions?

Tag questions are phrases like, "can't you?" that are added to the end of a statement. They help the statement get by the conscious mind by occupying the mind with the tag question.

Since the question elicits some transderivational searching, it also helps with the trance.

Drug companies do something like this in their advertising in order to make the information about side effects of drugs less noticeable. That is an unfortunate use of a valuable tool.

Here are some example statements with tag questions: As you think of these successes, you can let your mind go to early memories of success, can't you? You have memories of special things you can do, do you not? And this strong foundation of early learning and success is part of how you feel, isn't it?

# What are Double Binds?

In double binds that are therapeutic or motivational, you give the person a choice between two forms of the very same presupposition. For example, you might say, "These memories of success can come up with your help, or run through your subconscious on their own, I don't know which one your subconscious will choose."

As you heard, we added a vague statement of uncertainty about your subconscious choosing one of the options. This reduces the sense of coercion, generates some transderivational search for increased trance, and makes the sense of having options less stressful. It's part of using language in a way that feels less like working though information, and more like floating.

# What are Embedded Commands?

Embedded commands are statements that are inserted into larger sentences. You may notice embedded commands more and more as you hear them in this training.

Did you hear the ones I just used?

I said, "notice embedded commands more and more," and I said, "hear them in this training." Listen as I say the whole sentence again: "You may notice embedded commands more and more as you hear them in this training." You heard them this time, didn't you? As you >>practice this technique, you will >>find yourself able to >>use embedded commands in many situations.

# What is Analogue Marking?

Erickson would change the way he said the embedded commands that he was sending into the subconscious.

This marked them in a way that was not too obvious, but helped them function as influential entities all on their own. >>You can do this when >>you speak persuasively to >>influence others.

# What is Utilization?

Utilization is a technique that has opened up entirely new vistas in mental health treatment and personal life. Utilization happens when you turn an existing resource into a tool for a meaningful purpose. Where this can be surprising is when things that seem very negative or inappropriate are used, or repurposed.

Often, the negative behavior is just a dysfunctional attempt to get a good outcome, as when a child misbehaves because it gets them some attention.

When Erickson was working at a mental hospital, there was a patient there who claimed to be Jesus Christ. The patient spent quite a bit of time rubbing his hands together while he was spaced out. It also happens that the hospital had a wood shop where patients could do projects. Once day, Erickson approached the patient and said, "Sir, I understand you are a carpenter." Since Jesus is well-known to have been a carpenter, Erickson knew that the patient would have to say yes, that he was a carpenter.

Erickson got him to cooperate with having sand paper and a wood block attached to his hands so that instead of merely rubbing his hands together, he would sand the block of wood.

In time, this sensory experience created familiarity, and his skills and interest became stronger. In time, this patient, who had seemed to be a hopeless case, was making furniture.

So what was it that Erickson utilized? He utilized the two most serious symptoms, symptoms that most other professionals would have attempted to eliminate: the delusion of being Jesus, and the long periods of being spaced out and uselessly rubbing his hands together. Erickson used these symptoms to link the patient with valuable resources: identity, motivation, engagement, and experience, as well as the real-world resource of the wood shop.

Next time you are concerned, disturbed, or just irritated by something that someone else is doing, put your creative hat on and see what creative forms of utilization you can come up with. Do brainstorming with other people who are also concerned for even more ideas and practical ways to put them into action. You can do utilization with difficult or troubled children as well.

# What is Nesting?

Nesting means that an idea is contained within another. That can happen in the form of a story that occurs within another story. The purpose is to enhance trance and open-mindedness.

It makes the metaphors or teaching elements of the story more powerful. When I was learning hypnosis, one of my teachers told us about when he was in Italy, and he was seeing so much art and architecture, and learning so much, that he had a dream where he was in a big Catholic church, and Mother Mary came down into the church on this sunbeam that glistened and radiated through the huge, beautiful and colorful stained glass window. She told him about giving birth, and the exquisite joy that she felt being part of history and a new movement that promised to make a better world, that the pain of childbirth and the humbleness of her surroundings could not compare with the kindness of her people.

This is about the memories as told by someone in a dream as told by someone in another country in a story about my training. That is four levels deep. My story (recalling training), the trainer's story (being in Italy), the dream (of the big church) and another story (Mother Mary's recollections). The story served as a container for metaphors about making changes in one's life despite the discomfort that can be part of that. The metaphor was of childbirth.

# What are Extended Quotes?

Extended quotes are a type of nesting where you have nested quotations. The example I just gave is a rich version of extended quotes, because each layer involves someone talking. The story was four levels, but involved only one nested quote, which was the trainer telling us what Mary said.

Even a simple version can enhance trance.

Although hearing something third or fourth hand should mean it has less credibility, filling someone's mind with credible or interesting people can have the opposite effect of making something more believable and desirable.

# Spell Out Words?

Spelling out an important word draws the person's attention to it, and promotes t-r-a-n-c-e.

# What is Conversational Postulate?

When someone asks you if you can pass the salt, they are actually asking you to pass the salt, but they're being nice about it. NLP calls this a conversational postulate. In hypnosis, this avoids creating resistance, and it generates a subconscious drive to act on the question.

Here are some examples.

"Can you imagine doing that?"

"Would you invite that area to relax?"

"How easily can you let your subconscious mind do this for you?"

You can use this structure in day-to-day business. "Are you prepared to use us as a vendor?" wouldn't exert a magic mind power over a potential customer, but it would be part of a persuasive communication pattern and attractive bid to the customer.

# What are Selectional Restriction Violations?

In the course of eliciting a state or creating a metaphor, you can ascribe feelings to things. This is called selectional restriction violation. Doing this not only furthers the metaphor, or supports the state, but it also contributes to trance and open-mindedness.

"Your lower back would like to absorb and store all that extra agitation you have been feeling, and create a balanced sense of your energies."

"What if your media player could tell you about all the wisdom and ideas for success that it will ever hold."

"The cactus lives peacefully in the arid desert."

# What are Ambiguities?

Part of Erickson's approach to working with trance states, was to take advantage of the opportunities afforded by ambiguity.

The double meaning of a vague phrase can contribute to trance, because of the transderivational searching that results.

The double meanings also can draw the attention toward a theme, but subconsciously, and can encourage a state be bringing up related material.

# What are Phonological Ambiguities?

You can take advantage of similarities of sound between words in creating ambiguity. Phonological ambiguity is uncertainty created by similar-sounding words.

"Can you be a good support about this?" (Sounds like good sport.)

"Relaxing from your head on down to your sole-s of your feet." (Sounds like down to your soul, spelled s-o-u-l instead of s-o-l-e.)

# What are Syntactic Ambiguities?

You can create ambiguity through violations of syntax. Now we're talking about actual grammar syntax, meaning word order. Syntax ambiguity means that the meaning of the statement is not readily clear because the syntax does not do the job it normally does of clarifying meaning.

You can easily create examples by taking a participle, that is, an -ing word, and a verb.

For example, "Deeply comforting psychotherapy clients cause success." What do you think, am I saying that clients become successful by developing comforting personalities? Or is it that learning to self-sooth creates success through greater emotional stability? Or is it simply that when you comfort them, this leads to success? Add to that that the -ing word, "comforting", could be a verb or an adjective.

Consider all the transderivational searching packed into that simple, short sentence. And as for state elicitation, all three of these interpretations have to do with comfort and success, and the pathway to success.

If you want the client to develop a state and mental direction that is about that, then this technique should help create those things.

# What are Scope Ambiguities?

In scope ambiguities, you wonder what part of the sentence applies to what other part.

For example, "When you are talking quietly with your child and your husband at ease to talk more openly..."

Does this mean she is talking quietly with her child and her husband, and SHE is becoming more open, or is it the husband who is becoming more open?

I'll say it again, "When you are talking quietly with your child and your husband at ease to talk more openly..." This could be part of a session intended to help her become ready for her husband to be more honest with her. In any case, consider how this ambiguity creates transderivational searching for meaning, and primes a state and interest in a topic.

# What are Punctuation Ambiguities?

You can create transderivational searches with punctuation ambiguities. One form is to blend sentences.

For example, "As you sense some of the excitement of learning physically sensing calm alertness." This is a sentence where the word "physically" does double duty in the middle of two clauses, one about physically sensing excitement, and the other about physically sensing calm alertness.

You can also add improper pauses like... this... as you experience... transderivational searching causing... you to try mind reading. These pauses can help you pace the person's breath as well.

Another punctuation ambiguity is created by not providing the end of the... As you do a transderivational search, into which I blend a new idea.

# What is a Metaphor?

The subconscious is always looking for solutions, but our defenses and traumas can keep us from connecting the dots. We have evolved to digest our daily experience through REM sleep, but traumatic and other anxiety-provoking material can prevent REM sleep from doing its job. However it is that we become stuck, one of the solutions to being stuck lies in the art of metaphor.

**Metaphor means creating a story or idea that symbolizes something.**

For example, you might write a story about a famous event in history, but change the characters into various mythological or magic characters. Many of the most famous stories are actually metaphors for what was going on politically at the time they were written. Many more are love stories that resemble our own love lives in various ways. That's why we can relate to them.

But Erickson contributed a great deal to using metaphor for healing. Metaphor bypasses the conscious mind, and helps the subconscious process issues that are stuck. Metaphor can help us process things that we did not process on our own.

The book Little Annie Stories is a wonderful collection of metaphorical stories to tell children that is intended to help them deal with difficult issues like bed wetting. The book My Voice Will Go With You: The Teaching Tales of Milton H. Erickson, M.D. is an excellent addition to the library of anyone interested in the Milton model and metaphor.

One way to begin building metaphors is to read collections of them; that is why I recommended those books. Of course there are others. You can begin building metaphors by picking a challenging issue, and changing it into a story about animals. Whatever the challenge is, turn it into something that has a similar emotional significance. For example, if the challenge is about regaining self esteem after a failure, the story could be about the animals going to a dried up watering hole, and going on a search for water.

The thing that makes a metaphor healing, is that there is some kind of healing message embedded in the story.

In the water metaphor, the animals going on a quest for water is like someone not being stuck in low self esteem, and going for new opportunities. Being thirsty didn't stop the animals; it drove them on.

Having a failure doesn't stop people, it drives them to build the needed skills and seek new challenges.

So the water is the metaphor for success and self esteem at the same time. Since people have parts, as we have learned, different characters in the story can match different parts. One of the animals could say, "It's hopeless, there's no point in going on, we must stay here and hope for rain."

The ensuing dialogue could be a message to the subconscious to turn the voice of hopelessness into a voice for motivation.

# What is the Satir Model?

Virginia Satir was one of the first family therapists. Like Erickson, she was modeled for NLP purposes, and her work is one of the three fundamental models of NLP. She was born in 1916 and became a noted psychotherapist.

Her best known books were Conjoint Family Therapy and Peoplemaking in which she describes her family therapy work to a popular audience. Satir wrote the book Changing With Families: A Book About Further Education for Being Human with Bandler and Grinder.

She developed the Virginia Satir Change Process Model through clinical studies. This model has also been applied to organizational change.

# What are the Satir Categories?

Satir found that people fell into five categories, each of which had its own body language, attitude, and communication patterns. They are the Blamer, Placater, Computer, Distracter and Leveler. NLP has incorporated these styles into its trainings.

I'll go over the basics on each one.

# Who is The Blamer?

Blamer's externalize blame, and appear to be always ready to place the blame in a harsh or judgmental way. When things go wrong, the blamer starts blaming.

The blamer also pushes their thoughts and feelings onto everyone else. In NLP, you may see blamers referred to as skunks, because they spray their criticism outward.

Blamers, like all the categories, have their own body language. When they're in blaming mode, they point their finger at people and have a firm, controlling style of body language.

They tend to use confusion tactics to make it easier to get the blame to stick without too much resistance from others.

They do this with meta-model violations such as overgeneralizing, connecting ideas that don't belong together, and making claims for which there is no proof.

Blamers can end up being pretty lonely, because their behavior is alienating.

They do best with very like-minded people and stay at peace with them by focusing their blame on the same people or groups. This forms a kind of bond.

Inside, the blamer may not be nearly as confident and secure as they appear.

Blaming can serve to compensate for vulnerabilities such as the fear of judgement, and feeling so small as to need to align with a larger authority that justifies being blaming in service of that larger authority. Blamers generally blame in the name of a system such as family, church, employer or political cause. As an employer or supervisor, they may blame in the name of profit. Blame can be a strategy for office politics.

Blamers use general statements, complex comparisons and missing proofs to confuse the other person, and then place the blame. Such people usually end up alone, since nobody wants to be at the receiving end of the blame.

# Who is The Placater?

The placater is also one for displacing blame, but they do it more diplomatically. The placater is much more concerned about how people view them, so much of their behavior is an escape from conflict or unwanted attention or blame.

A blamer will fight fire with fire, but a placater blows the fire onto someone else's house and shares their neighbor's upset over the fire department being slow to arrive. Their body language tends to be palms facing up and shoulders shrugging, they may tend to slouch.

Placaters hide their approach with meta-model violations such as cause and effect, modal operators and unspecified verbs. They may get your sympathy with a poor-me attitude. When there is conflict, they go into hiding, at least by becoming noncommittal. Placaters may be found firmly sitting on the fence.

# Who is The Computer?

The computer style can be pretty unemotional. They cover up possible emotions with extra words. They may sound academic or scientific.

When someone else becomes emotional, they act like they are trying to become a counter-weight, by acting even more cool, calm, and collected. Computers hide from their own feelings and invalidate other's feelings, because they have not learned to cope with feelings, whether the feelings are their own or someone else's.

NLP trainings have referred to them as Mr. Cool, or Mr. Spock, a science fiction character from a planet where everyone aspired to be perfectly logical.

They may tend to fold their arms, especially when things get too personal for them, and they are often seen in a neutral posture.

Some fit the nerd stereotype, and may be physically awkward or make gestures that are a bit eccentric or un-selfconscious. It may seem like they are drawing their energy up into their head, and that their body mostly serves to support their brain.

In relationships, the computer can harm the intimacy by being too far removed. Many computer style people are considered to have an autism spectrum diagnosis such as Asperger syndrome.

In terms of meta-model patterns, computers hide by using generalizations and omitting references.

# Who is The Distracter?

There is another style that can be a chameleon. They are seen as a mix of blamer, computer, and placater. But there is a common thread that runs through their style, and that is to manipulate through distraction.

They may induce confusion or simple fatigue in the other person.

They train others not to hold them accountable by making it very difficult to have a straight conversation with them. They are intuitive about escalating the distraction as needed.

They can be quite exasperating, especially if they are not very socially skilled or if they are cognitively impaired.

They may tend to gesture a great deal in an attempt to communicate their thoughts and emotions with their body, but subconsciously, this can serve to further fill up other people with excess stimuli for adding to the confusion.

From a meta-model point of view, they switch topics too much, overgeneralize, and omit references.

# Who is The Leveler?

Finally, there is the leveler. The leveler has high congruence and does not blanch at being factual. They do not over-dramatize, so if there is blaming to do, they are objective and fair about it.

When confronted by the other styles, the most evolved levelers have a special ability to stay in touch with reality and their own agenda and self-interest.

If they upset anyone, it's because their style interferes with manipulation by the other styles. What upsets people more than someone getting in the way of their attempts to manipulate?

The leveler may have their hands facing down, as if they are trying to calm things down and encourage level-headedness. This is because they often end up in a mediator role because of their own level-headedness. Their ability to see both sides of an argument makes them good mediators.

# What about Flexibility?

An important part of the Satir model is that people need to develop flexibility in their styles, so that they are not locked into one.

With more flexibility, people can adapt to more situations, and can solve more interpersonal problems.

They can certainly create less personal problems with that flexibility. So while the leveler sounds like the best style, it can be a problem if it is the only style you are comfortable in.

A good mediator knows that having various styles can make the difference between success and failure in a negotiation.

The same holds true for anyone, really.

For example, being a blamer may help knock someone off of a stuck position, because it is a real state interrupt. It may help level the playing field when someone else is being too high-handed.

# What is Category Rapport-Building?

Done properly, you may actually win the respect of a blamer by acting like a blamer, but this is advanced.

You have to be in that style without putting the blamer on the defensive, so pacing the blamer style means adopting that kind of critical attitude and intensity WITHOUT causing the blamer to feel that they must fight with you or otherwise defend their vulnerability.

Being upset about the same thing as the blamer is an excellent strategy. Remember that after pacing comes leading. The blamer is much more open to your input once rapport has been established. The problem for most people is that they are too shaken up or angry to want to establish rapport with a blamer.

Since blamers may hold a lot of power in an organization, this can be a fatal mistake. It's best to see it as an opportunity to practice NLP rather than to practice your vulnerability. Which do you love more?

You can gain rapport with a placater pretty easily, since they really crave attention and understanding. The trick is to get them connected with their real responsibilities without losing them.

Starting with their higher values, that is, at a more general or abstract level and working down into the specifics is an excellent strategy.

Distracters are more open to rapport-building than you might think. As with most rapport-building, you must start out being non-threatening. Being non-threatening with a Satir category means not directly confronting the way the style acts as a defense against internal vulnerabilities.

In the case of the distracter, you do not rub their face in whatever it was they were trying to distract you from. As an NLP practitioner, you are getting used to juggling different ideas and even using confusion as a technique yourself.

The trick with the distracter is to lock firmly onto the facts and position and agenda that are important to you, and then take a detour. Go all over the place with the distracter, but keep dropping in points about how it is in the best interest of the distracter to do what must be done. It's a bit like breaking a horse.

While the distracter tends to fatigue others, you are fatiguing the distracter because all their efforts keep bringing them back to the same spot, your agenda. On one level, you are pacing them; on another, you are kindling a state of compliance. Add Ericksonian language to the free-wheeling conversation and you will be the distracter master.

Since levelers respect other levelers, and your NLP skills help you see both sides to any debate, you will have the easiest time establishing rapport and understanding with the leveler. If there is a disagreement, make sure that you have good mastery of the facts and good knowledge of the agendas of the players in the situation.

Of course, you can use everything you had already learned about rapport-building. But now you know even more. By learning about the Satir categories, you know not only more about what to do, but also about what to avoid doing.

But if you aren't sure where to start in an interaction, being the leveler is best. That's because the leveler always understands their side of the issue.

The only concern is that the leveler may be persuaded by the other side. This creates an incentive - for the person you are talking to - to want to create rapport.

If they are not skilled, or if they are stressed, they may fall into their more un-evolved category style, but that means that they will be more obvious as to what category they belong to.

You will be able to take your cues from there. It is

very important to remember that when you see someone in a more stereotypical or manipulative or irrational state, that may not be where they are most of the time, so don't limit yourself by assuming that what you see is all you will be dealing with in the future. People who see this have an easier time bringing out the best in people. This makes their lives a lot easier.

# One more: Why isn't NLP a mainstream approach?

**Written By: Rasa Galatiltyte**

There you have it. This is one of the most difficult, if not THE most disturbing, questions to answer. As active practitioners in the field, we get this question quite a lot. Mostly, from other NLP advocates! Rarely a client would come in and ask such questions. Since you bought this book and kept reading beyond the first few pages, here is an answer that should / could / would (we hope) ease your mind.

Here is a known fact:

Neuro Linguistic Programming has had a significant influence on psychotherapy, counseling, sales, coaching, leadership, and plenty of other professional fields. Trainers and therapists have borrowed techniques from Neuro Linguistic Programming or been influenced by it. However, Neuro Linguistic Programming has not gained a lasting place in academic work, and few mainstream therapists acknowledge it.

There are several primary reasons.

One reason is that it attracted very diverse, and not always competent or honest advocates. We know some of these people, do we not? Another reason is that serious academic research institutes and leaders were not supportive of NLP, for their own reasons.

Unfortunately, researchers focused on the wrong things. They chose aspects that were easy to research, but didn't really represent NLP. Also, a fair amount of the initial writings on NLP (excluding The Structure Of Magic, volume I and II) was mostly for self-help and less-academically-educated readers, and there was no widely accepted central body to establish standards.

Because the most central fundamental nature of Neuro Linguistic Programming is as a means of modeling and creating training, it was destined to sprout offshoots that were quite diverse.

On top of this, people tend to confuse NLP with the techniques that come from it. They get the impression that NLP has no cohesive identity or that it is just a way to promote success seminars or hypnotize people. We had the same conception of this field before studying it thoroughly.

We are not going to point fingers and blame anyone for that unfortunate development. Who's fault it is and why it had to come about this way – these are questions for historians, not for therapists. The average self-help seeker jumped on the NLP-training-wagon instantly.

This was certainly the same impression that academics got. They looked for clear-cut ideas, but found in NLP a mish-mash of unscientific thinking that obscured the essence and contributions of NLP. For them, there was no "there" there. The result is that many therapists use techniques that have sprouted from NLP, but without knowing (or acknowledging) where it came from. This has left NLP to be identified with the more outlandish or marginalized practitioners, or simply disregarded or forgotten.

Much of the writing of NLP practitioners also detracted from its credibility because it had a scattered or pedantic style. It appears that NLP's emphasis on innovation, "bite-sized" techniques, and grandiose promises tended to attract people with unaddressed symptoms of attention deficit disorder (ADD/ADHD) or other problems in need of insight. This seems to have produced a self-perpetuating cycle that sealed the fate of NLP in so far as the mainstream is concerned.

This meant that the greatest assets left to promote NLP were the clients of the NLP practitioners. Their voices, though largely positive, were not collectively strong enough to propel NLP into a status as lasting as cognitive psychotherapy, but NLP did have a strong wave of interest that lasted roughly twenty years.

Ok, we are not here to cry over the past or protest or smash any researcher's door (or window). We are here to learn how to help our clients better and "do NLP" the right way. Perhaps, as time goes by and more clients reach their outcomes, the mainstream mental health field will acknowledge and recognize the enormous contribution we all had to their own professional growth.

We now know that many concepts that found their way into Neuro Linguistic Programming training, some more than four decades ago, were not really supported by adequate observation, experience, or scientific understanding.

Nonetheless, you can still find a lot of those outdated old-fashioned concepts and methodologies in many NLP programs today. This is testimony to the power of traditions, groupthink, and wishful thinking. In contrast, this book you're holding brings the core assumptions and functions of NLP into the foreground, showing them at work in modern practices.

We hope you find that it makes NLP more accessible as it provides fresh techniques and explanations that expand your repertoire in a scientifically defensible way. What we remind ourselves every day are the words of Richard Bandler, the famous co-founder of Neuro Linguistic Programming:

**"NLP is an attitude and a methodology that leaves behind a trail of techniques."**

Any attitudes and methodologies are bound to improve and change in time. We truly believe that now is the best time to acknowledge that fact and take a new perspective when studying this field.

# What else?

That's it! You now own the basic knowledge and skills of Neuro Linguistic Programming.

I hope you enjoyed this book and I'm really interested to hear your comments and experiences.

Come visit us at NLPWeeklyMagazine.com. You will find a lot of free resources, many techniques and the largest most passionate and warm NLP community, ready to support you at any time.

If you'd like to learn the full scope of NLP techniques and methods, get a copy of my other book, **"The Big Book of NLP, Expanded: 350+ Techniques, Patterns & Strategies of Neuro Linguistic Programming"**.

Thank you again for reading and let's get started!

Please send your comments to:

editor@nlpweeklymagazine.com

"A man's character may be learned from the adjectives which he habitually uses in conversation."

- Mark Twain